POWER PRAYERS

Praying

YOUR KIDS

POWER PRAYERS

Praying for

YOUR KIDS

JANICE THOMPSON

BARBOUR BOOKS
An Imprint of Barbour Publishing, Inc.

Dedication

For my eight grandchildren: Maddy, Ethan,
Peyton, Brooke, Jenna, Avery, Boston, and Harper.
Nina loves you very much and dedicates this book to you.

Acknowledgments

Special thanks to Janet Kilchine, Mary LeJune,
and Karen Bailey, who offered to read the book from cover
to cover before I turned it in. Thanks for your help, ladies!

Contents

Covering Your Children in Prayer

What a wonderful privilege, to pray for our children. They are entrusted to us for such a short time. When we recognize this, we take our prayer time very seriously. Not that we only pray about the serious things, of course. If you're a parent, you've probably spent hours praying for MIA homework assignments, lost toys, missing shoes, and scraped knees. Likely you've also prayed for pet frogs, sick hamsters, and invisible friends.

Our prayers for our children don't have to be complex or time consuming. (Not many parents have extra time on their hands, after all.) A steady stream of heartfelt words to our heavenly Father about those precious, precocious kiddos is essential, even if they're spoken in the shower or while driving home from work.

Why are our prayers for our children so essential? Perhaps we should think of them as an umbrella. They provide a covering for our kids, a protection. We wouldn't send our children out into a rainstorm without an umbrella or raincoat. Neither should we send them out into this world without protection. They need it during the formative years, and they need it when they're grown. Our prayers for our children never stop, no matter their age. Many of us, whose parents are still alive, know this to be true. They're praying for us right now!

How should we pray, specifically? There are so many areas where we need to dig in our heels and cover our children. This book will serve as a guide, giving you prayer prompts for issues like faith, trust, purity, wisdom, dreams and goals, and many more. You will be encouraged to pray for your child's work ethic, diligence, generosity, and even his future spouse (though most parents aren't ready to think about that one just yet).

Whether you have five minutes to pray or an hour, you can pray powerfully.

How to use this book:

Power Prayers: Praying for your Kids will help you pray more effectively for your children. Each chapter contains a brief overview of an important prayer focus to help shape their young lives. The balance of each chapter includes "starter prayers" you can use in your own prayer time. The prayers are divided by topic (twenty-one total) and each topic has fourteen different prayer starters. Because we're praying for both boys and girls, the prayers go back and forth from *he* to *she*, so that everyone will feel included. If you're the parent of a son, feel free to change the pronouns to *he*. If you're the parent of a daughter, the *he's* can become *she's*. In other words, this is your book to use as you see fit. Your prayers have the power to change your child's life! May this book find a permanent place in your home as you raise your child to love the Lord.

Are you ready to embark on a journey of praying powerfully? Let's get started!

This is the confidence we have in approaching God:
that if we ask anything according to his will, he hears us.
1 JOHN 5:14 NIV

CHAPTER ONE

Purity

——

God's kids are called to walk in purity, to set an example for their peers. This has always been tough, but never more so than now. Today's children are confronted at every turn with images they shouldn't see, songs they shouldn't hear, and news stories that threaten to weaken their defenses. Television shows, movies, music lyrics, and even TV commercials blast one impurity after another, and it's hard to defend against them. That's why it's more important than ever to pray for your child's purity during their formative years. They need your spiritual covering in order to remain pure.

Perhaps you've settled on the idea that it's just sexual purity God is looking for. Truth is, He longs for us to be pure in our thoughts, our attitudes, our relationships, and our actions. This extends far beyond what we usually think. Our child's purity isn't just about how she dresses. It's not about keeping her away from the opposite sex. It's about the things she sees, the things she says, the songs she's listening to on the radio, and the attitudes she exhibits. Purity is truly a heart issue, not just an external issue. Because most people don't see it this way, the issue is rarely addressed comprehensively.

So, how can we, as parents, pray for our kids when they're confronted on every side? Is there really a way to protect them? Is our prayer umbrella wide enough to do the job? According to God's Word, prayer is the best possible defense. It's our number one weapon. We must pray for God to guard our children's hearts, to protect their eyes and ears. We must also pray for peers who will commit to joining them as sons and daughters dedicated to living holy lives. This might sound impossible, but remember, God delights in doing the impossible. It brings Him great joy, in fact.

Our prayers for our children (no matter their age) should be consistent, day in and day out. We can't give up when they're off on a tangent, doing things they shouldn't. In fact, we need to dig in our heels and pray even harder during these seasons. We can't get lazy when they're coasting along, doing fine, either. We must commit ourselves to lifting them up as they head to school, to the neighbor's house, to their ball games, to the movies. There's never a situation where we should lift our prayer covering.

We need to do all we can to protect our children, but ultimately they will be the ones making the decisions about their purity level. We can train them. We can lead by example. Yet we can't make them be pure. Why? Because we have no control over what goes on inside of the heart. That's why we lean so much on the Lord. Only He can whisper "Slow down, kiddo" when our child is about to step out of the safety zone. A heart that beats in sync with the Lord's is a heart that longs for purity. When our children move out from under the umbrella of His presence, they're more likely to dabble in things they shouldn't. So, keep them close, parents! Time in God's presence trumps any lecture you can give about purity, after all. In that holy place, God can do the convincing.

It's time to pray, but before you do, examine your own heart. Make sure you're in a place of purity—in thoughts, words, and deeds—before you intercede for your child. Then ask the Lord to swing wide the door of grace and to speak clearly to your child that his heart may be pure.

Such as These

Jesus said, "Let the little children come to me, and do not hinder them, for the kingdom of heaven belongs to such as these."
MATTHEW 19:14 NIV

Father, I know that You love my child even more than I do (which must be a lot!). Your greatest desire is for her to love You and walk in Your ways. Today I ask that You draw her to You so that she will feel Your heartbeat. May she always recognize Your voice. May she long to please You and to walk in purity and grace all of her days. Amen.

A Way of Escape

No temptation has overtaken you that is not common to man. God is faithful, and he will not let you be tempted beyond your ability, but with the temptation he will also provide the way of escape, that you may be able to endure it.
1 CORINTHIANS 10:13 ESV

Lord, there are so many voices out there calling out to my child. I know he will be tempted time and time again. I ask, Lord, that You give him the strength to rise above any temptation. May he walk in purity all of his days, Father—not just physically, but in his thoughts, his attitude, his actions. When he's tempted, Lord, please remind him every time that there is a way of escape. Amen.

Shifting Our Gaze

Turn my eyes from looking at worthless things;
and give me life in your ways.
PSALM 119:37 ESV

What a crazy world we live in, Father! With the Internet, television, movies, and all of the other distractions life has to offer, I know that my child has a lot to look at, a lot to take in. Most of it is a waste of his time, a distraction. I'm asking today that You guard his heart, so that the worthless things don't hold his attention. Rivet his attention on You, Lord, and not on meaningless things that seek to draw him in. Amen.

Steady Steps

Keep steady my steps according to your promise,
and let no iniquity get dominion over me.
PSALM 119:133 ESV

Father, we all need a daily reminder that we can walk in Your ways. . . in the moment. Distractions will come, and our feet will be tempted to wander in a different direction, but You draw us back each time, as we call out to You. Today I ask You to speak softly to my child's heart, so that she will know Your voice and guard her footsteps. May she walk in Your ways, even during trying times, Lord. May every step be guided by You.

Elevated Thoughts

Set your minds on things that are above,
not on things that are on earth.
COLOSSIANS 3:2 ESV

So many things to think about, Lord! I know my child is torn in so many directions as her thoughts shift from school to relationships to playtime. Sometimes she gets bogged down. I ask today that You elevate her thoughts. Your Word says that she can set her mind on things above. I ask that You help her with that process, Lord. Shift her gaze to You and not the things in front of her, especially when she's hurting or facing problems. Remind her today to keep her eyes on You and not the things she sees. Amen.

Dressed for Success

But put on the Lord Jesus Christ,
and make no provision for the flesh,
to gratify its desires.
ROMANS 13:14 ESV

Father, so much emphasis is put on how kids dress these days. I've watched my child compare herself to others, and it often breaks my heart. Remind her today that the very best way to dress herself for success is to "put on" You each day—to spend time in Your presence and in Your Word. There is no article of clothing that even comes close to a pure heart, kind words, and a generous spirit. She can have all of that, if she resides in You. May she always remain dressed for true success, Lord.

Think on These Things

Finally, brothers, whatever is true, whatever is honorable,
whatever is just, whatever is pure, whatever is lovely,
whatever is commendable, if there is any excellence,
if there is anything worthy of praise, think about these things.
PHILIPPIANS 4:8 ESV

Lord, thank You that You care so much about the things my child thinks about. You have a plan for his thinking—from the time he wakes up till the time he goes to bed. I'm so grateful that You can turn his thoughts to things that are honorable. Just. Commendable. True. Knowing You are interested in his thought life brings me such peace, Father! I rest easy knowing You've got this. Amen.

Going into the Sanctuary

All in vain have I kept my heart clean and washed my
hands in innocence. For all the day long I have been stricken
and rebuked every morning. If I had said, "I will speak thus,"
I would have betrayed the generation of your children.
But when I thought how to understand this, it seemed to me a wearisome task,
until I went into the sanctuary of God; then I discerned their end.
PSALM 73:13–17 ESV

Lord, I know that true purity comes from having a heart after You, and I also know that keeping my child's eyes on You means I should keep her focused on her prayer time. Show me how to draw her into the sanctuary on a daily basis. I also know how critical it is to be in fellowship with other believers who are like-minded so that she can learn from others' example, even when outside the home. Thank You for giving our family wisdom so that we can be in a church environment where Your name is lifted high and my child's heart is safe. Amen.

Crucified with Christ

*I have been crucified with Christ. It is no longer I who live,
but Christ who lives in me. And the life I now live in the flesh I live
by faith in the Son of God, who loved me and gave himself for me.*
GALATIANS 2:20 ESV

Lord, as an adult I understand what it means to crucify the flesh. It seems I'm doing it all the time. I ask that You teach my child what it means to die to his flesh, to lay down impure thoughts and desires so that he can live—fully live—as You have called him to, with absolute purity. Draw Him with Your Spirit, Father, so that he recognizes Your voice and learns to rely on Your power and not his own. Amen.

No Wandering Allowed

*How can a young man keep his way pure?
By guarding it according to your word. With my whole heart I seek you;
let me not wander from your commandments!*
PSALM 119:9–10 ESV

Lord, I know what it's like to wander. I've done a little of that in my life. I don't want my children to make the same mistakes I made. I ask that You illuminate their path so that they walk in Your ways. . . always. This narrow path will keep them pure, Lord. Their focus will remain on the goal (You) and not the distractions (impurities). Set their feet on a good road, Father. No stumbling. No veering off the path. Just straight into Your arms, where they will be blessed. Amen.

Create in Me

Create in me a clean heart, O God,
and renew a right spirit within me.
PSALM 51:10 ESV

Father, how creative You are! All we have to do is look around at the animals, the trees, the flowers, and we see that Your works are amazing. How much more You must care about my child's heart, Lord. You're doing a creative work there, too! I see it more and more as the days go by. She comes in contact with so many things that threaten to undo Your work, but no weapon formed against her will prosper. You're creating a clean heart inside of her, and I'm so very grateful! Amen.

———

A Person of Honor

Pray for us, for we are sure that we have a clear conscience,
desiring to act honorably in all things.
HEBREWS 13:18 ESV

Honorable actions. How we need them, Lord! We need to be honorable in all we do, not just when others are watching but when we are alone. Today I pray that my child's walk toward purity would include honorable actions. When speaking to adults. When hanging out with peers. When alone. In his thoughts. In his prayer time. May everything he does bring honor, Father, not just now but as he grows into a wonderful man of God. Amen!

A Fine Example

Let no one despise you for your youth, but set the believers
an example in speech, in conduct, in love, in faith, in purity.
1 TIMOTHY 4:12 ESV

I remember what it was like to be young, Lord. Well, mostly. Sometimes children don't feel like they're leaders. They're insecure because of their age, or maybe they're made to feel that their thoughts and ideas aren't as valuable because they're young. Today, please whisper to my child's heart. Remind her that she's a leader! She's an example for others (even for a few of the adults in her life). Show her how to step up and lead with conviction and grace. Amen.

Faithful and Just

If we confess our sins, he is faithful and just to forgive us
our sins and to cleanse us from all unrighteousness.
1 JOHN 1:9 ESV

No one knows us better than we know ourselves. Except You, Lord. You know every dark secret. We all have them, unconfessed or not. Today I pray for my child. If he has hidden places, things he's done that break Your heart, shine Your light on those areas and restore his purity. Remind him that You are faithful and just to forgive every sin. You can give him a fresh start and cleanse him from all unrighteousness. Then set his feet on a right path—toward purity. Toward You. Amen.

CHAPTER TWO

Courage

—

Kids today know what it is to be brave. They're asked to exhibit courage at every turn (perhaps more than we ever had to at their age). The world is changing rapidly, and scary things confront them at every turn. No wonder so many children shy away from problems. It's a big, scary world out there! It's easier to close your eyes and pretend problems don't exist. Right?

To be courageous doesn't mean your child won't ever be afraid. To be courageous means he can face those fears head on and do something about them. He can square his shoulders, look fear in the eye, and step out in faith. He's little David facing the mighty Goliath. He's Peter walking on the water. He's Nehemiah rebuilding the wall. He's an Israelite crossing the Red Sea on dry land.

Of course, this is easier said than done. Sometimes he feels more like Job, defeated and alone. Why does his courage wane? For most of us, courage comes and goes, depending on our depth of relationship with the Lord at any given moment. When we're close to Him, when we feel His heartbeat, we feel strong. When we step away, we feel weak.

Courage comes from a deep, abiding assurance that God is for us, not against us—that He will come out swinging on our behalf. His power (the same power that propelled Jesus from the grave) resides inside of us, even when we're facing really scary things. Our children can have that same power. They can. It's not just meant for adults. They need to learn by example. When you're courageous, you don't sit back. You step out. When you're courageous, you don't depend on your own ability. You rest in God's ability. Courage is not something you think about. It's something you do.

How do you model courage? You don't cower when trials come. You don't sink to the depths of despair when the enemy rears his head. You take some time to pray, to think. Then, with God's power residing inside of you, you square your shoulders and step out, convinced the Lord won't let you down. He won't, you know. He loves you (and your child) so much.

Perhaps the best way parents exhibit courage is by trusting God during their prayer time. They don't fret as they lift their child in prayer. They don't wonder if the Lord will come through for their kiddos. They trust completely. That trust spills over onto the whole family, causing everyone to be more courageous.

Your children are watching. So, pray first for courage for yourselves, parents. Then ask the Lord to bolster your child and prepare him for any battles ahead. They will come, but he can overcome them like the warrior he was meant to be. Amen?

Be Strong and Courageous

"Have I not commanded you? Be strong and courageous.
Do not be frightened, and do not be afraid,
for the LORD your God is with you wherever you go."
JOSHUA 1:9 ESV

Father, I know what it's like to live in fear. I've been down that road. I don't want that for my child. Whether she's at school, in the neighborhood, at church, or in the home, please give her the courage to face her Goliaths when they confront her. May she not cower in fear. While You're at it, Lord, increase my faith so that I can teach her by example. When our whole family is courageous, the children will be courageous. Thanks for the reminder that You are with us wherever we go. Amen.

Keep It Up!

"So keep up your courage, men, for I have faith
in God that it will happen just as he told me."
ACTS 27:25 NIV

I know what it's like to go up and down in my thought life, Lord. One minute I'm courageous, the next I'm shaking in my boots! It's as if I forget the things You've done in the past. May it not be so for my child. May he walk in courage, not just today when he's facing challenges with peers or studies, but may he make a daily choice to keep up his courage tomorrow and all the days ahead. What joy, to watch his faith grow as he overcomes hurdles. I'm so grateful, Lord! Amen.

I Am Here

But Jesus spoke to them at once. "Don't be afraid," he said.
"Take courage. I am here!"
MATTHEW 14:27 NLT

Oh, Father! There's something so comforting about knowing that You are here with us. Knowing You are right beside me gives me supernatural courage far beyond anything I could conjure up. I'm asking that You remind my child daily that You are here. . .right beside her at all times. When she's struggling with her grades, You are here. When she's feeling left out or lonely, You are here. When her courage wanes, You are here. May she come to recognize Your presence and then enjoy the surge of boldness that comes as a result. Amen.

Ordinary Men

When they saw the courage of Peter and John
and realized that they were unschooled, ordinary men,
they were astonished and they took note
that these men had been with Jesus.
ACTS 4:13 NIV

Father, sometimes my son goes through seasons where he feels ordinary. In fact, he sometimes feels "less than" the other boys. It breaks my heart. Then I'm reminded of this scripture. The disciples were "ordinary" men—mostly unschooled, at that. They had every reason to feel "less than," but You encouraged them to think beyond their limitations. May it be so with my son as well.

No Turning!

"Be strong and very courageous. Be careful to obey all the law my servant Moses gave you; do not turn from it to the right or to the left, that you may be successful wherever you go."
JOSHUA 1:7 NIV

Lord, I know what it's like to keep my eyes on the road while I'm driving. If I look to the right or left, I'm sure to cause an accident! The same is true in my faith walk. If I get distracted, I go off course. I've seen my children struggle in this area, too. Please help them stay focused on what Your Word says, Father, not what they see around them. When they refuse to turn their eyes from Your precepts, they remain courageous, and that's so important. You've helped me with my focus, Lord! I know You will help my children as well. Amen.

Not Forsaken

"Be strong and courageous. Do not be afraid or terrified because of them, for the LORD your God goes with you; he will never leave you nor forsake you."
DEUTERONOMY 31:6 NIV

Those feelings of being "forsaken" are very real, Father. Children all over the globe struggle with feeling that way as they face unthinkable obstacles. Today I pray for my children—and for all children, both near and far—that they would never feel forsaken. There's really only one way for that to happen. They need to stay in Your presence. I ask You to make Yourself real to them. Draw them with Your Spirit, Father, and keep them close to Your heart. Above all, when they're feeling afraid, please let that "nearness" serve as a reminder that they are never, ever alone. Amen.

Out with Discouragement!

*"Then you will have success if you are careful to observe the
decrees and laws that the LORD gave Moses for Israel.
Be strong and courageous. Do not be afraid or discouraged."*
1 CHRONICLES 22:13 NIV

Sometimes I get so discouraged when I turn on the news or pick up
a newspaper, Lord. So many frightening things are happening in the
world—it's enough to make a person's heart heavy. I've seen that same
heaviness in my child's heart when she gets overwhelmed. She tends
to want to hide away, and I understand that. Today, I ask that You
remind her that she doesn't have to live in discouragement. Take away
the "dis-" and leave only the—"courage" part, Father. She can be strong
and courageous if she disses the dis-, but that can only happen with
Your help. So, help her, Lord, I pray. Amen.

Brave

*The Israelites fought constantly with the Philistines throughout
Saul's lifetime. So whenever Saul observed a young man
who was brave and strong, he drafted him into his army.*
1 SAMUEL 14:52 NLT

Dear Lord, I know that You know what it's like to see your kids cower
in fear. You've seen a lot of it, from the beginning of time. You've also
seen plenty who are young and brave. Sometimes I think my son is a
little too brave! He dives into things without thinking. Yet You can
take a courageous heart (like his) and mold it and shape it into a strong
warrior for Your kingdom. That's what I ask for today, Father. Smooth
off the rough edges and use his bravery for good. Give him direction
and courage that match up, so that he can be effective for You, not just
today, but as he grows to be a man. Amen.

Want Courage? Be Patient!

Wait for the LORD; be strong,
and let your heart take courage; wait for the LORD!
PSALM 27:14 ESV

Patience is a virtue. I've heard that saying all of my life, Lord. We're told over and over again in scripture to be patient, but I never realized until reading this verse that patience propels us toward courage! My child needs this revelation, too, Father. He's often impatient, rushing when he should be slowing down. I pray that You would teach him this lesson—in Your own time, of course. Make him a patient man of courage. Amen.

Only Believe

But overhearing what they said, Jesus said to the
ruler of the synagogue, "Do not fear, only believe."
MARK 5:36 ESV

When I read the words "only believe" I can't help but think, "That sounds so simple!" However, I know it's not, Lord! *Only believing* is one of the hardest things to do. Why? Because I want to fix things. I want to step up and *do* something. To only believe means I place my full trust in You and not my own actions. I've seen my child struggle in this area, too. That's why I'm asking You to speak to her heart today. Whisper the words, "Only believe." Amen.

Newsworthy

He is not afraid of bad news;
his heart is firm, trusting in the LORD.
PSALM 112:7 ESV

It's so scary to turn on the news these days, Lord. It seems like every story is bad. We cringe, just thinking about the atrocities going on around the world. Our temptation, even for those of us who are strong in our faith, is to lose heart, to lose courage. This scripture is perfect, both for my child and for me! We both need the reminder that we don't have to be afraid of bad news. When we trust in You, You make our hearts firm. Bless You for that. Amen.

Walking on Water

He said, "Come." So Peter got out of the boat
and walked on the water and came to Jesus.
MATTHEW 14:29 ESV

My child faces situations that seem impossible to her. She looks at them and shakes her head and says, "There's just no way. I can't do that." I know the feeling. So did Peter, Your disciple. Yet You convinced him (and I know you can convince my child) that one bold step out of the boat can change everything. Today, Father, please teach my child to walk on the water. May she keep her eyes on You every step of the way. Amen.

We've Got the Power

But we have power over all these things
through Jesus who loves us so much.
ROMANS 8:37 NLV

Courage is a lot like a light bulb, isn't it, Lord? As long as it's plugged into the power source, it lights up! When we wander away from You, we lose our source of power. We grow weak. Today I commit to stay strong in You and to do the best I can to keep my children plugged in. My greatest desire is to model You so that they will know what it means to walk in genuine relationship with the King of kings. If we abide in You, we'll never be without power, Father. Thank You for that assurance. Amen.

Who Can Be Against Us?

What can we say about all these things?
Since God is for us, who can be against us?
ROMANS 8:31 NLV

You are for us, Lord. When we're going through joyous seasons, You're for us. When we are hurting, You're on our side. Nothing—absolutely nothing—can stand against us! It brings such peace to my heart to know that this applies to my child, too! You're for her, no matter what she's facing. Would You reveal that to her today, Father? If she's feeling like she has no one on her side, remind her that You are there, and You're never leaving. What comfort that will bring! Amen.

CHAPTER THREE

Joy

—

Joy is one of the many benefits of walking with the Lord. When we stay close to His heart, deep, abiding joy is ours. Sometimes we forget that our children are promised this same gift. We watch them struggle and wonder if they will ever be "happy." Their somber little faces make us sad. We do our best to counteract it with all sorts of things: treats, one-on-one time, special acknowledgments, and so on. Some of our attempts succeed. Others, not so much.

Happiness (by the world's standards) can never compare to what the Lord offers. No toy, no clothing item, no friendship can ever replace the kind of joy that God promises His kids. His version of joy has nothing to do with feelings. Of course, true joy results in happy feelings, but at its core, joy is rooted in trust. It's rooted in the security that God's got everything under control. When we know He's in control, we don't fret. When we're not fretting, we're more likely to relax and experience His version of joy.

Instead of just praying for your child to be happy, perhaps it would be better to pray, "Father, draw them close." Closeness assures peace, and true peace frees up joy. As it's freed, joy bubbles in much the same way detergent does when it hits water. More, more, more! That's how joy works for the child of God. More peace. More grace. More of all of the good things of God. All as a direct result of sticking close to the Author of joy, the One who gives it freely.

How do you model joy? Do you ignore bad behavior and laugh things off? No. Real joy isn't a fleeting feeling. It's something much deeper. It lasts much longer. Real joy says, "Today really stinks, but that's okay. God's on my side." Real joy still reaches out to others who are hurting, even when we ourselves are hurting. In other words, real joy has nothing to do with us. It has everything to do with Jesus. When we lean into Him, when we experience His goodness, His grace, His mercy, and His power, joy bubbles up. We can't stop it!

Here's a final nugget of truth: Don't pray for joy—for yourself or your child. Stop asking God to make you happy. Instead, pray for a deeper relationship with Jesus. Joy will come as a natural by-product of this. When it does, watch out! Your family, friends, and loved ones will all be affected!

So, what's holding you back? Step into His presence. Take your eyes off of your happiness, your child's happiness, your family's happiness. . .and focus solely on Him. Then, brace yourself for His abiding joy.

All Full!

"I have told you these things so that you will be
filled with my joy. Yes, your joy will overflow!"
JOHN 15:11 NLT

I know the experience of having a really great meal, Lord. . .being really, really full. There's such a sense of satisfaction, having my hunger filled. How much greater is the joy that comes when we're filled to the brim with Your love? I pray this very thing over my child today, Father. When he is reaching for literal food, give him a hunger for You. Fill him to overflowing so that joy—Your joy—will leave him completely satisfied, lacking nothing. What a blessing that will be in his life, Lord. Amen.

Enter with Singing

And those the LORD has rescued will return. They will enter Zion
with singing; everlasting joy will crown their heads.
Gladness and joy will overtake them, and sorrow and sighing will flee away.
ISAIAH 35:10 NIV

I love to watch my child sing praises to You, Lord. There's nothing sweeter to me than hearing her voice raised in worship. She has such a joyful, innocent heart. I know her song must thrill You as well. Best of all, her worship changes her heart and her situation. Praise emboldens her and reminds her of the great things You've done in her life. This thrills me! Like the Israelites entering their homeland with singing, I pray that she will enter the various situations in her life with as much enthusiasm and joy. Thank You for making this possible. Amen.

A Joy Sandwich

But the fruit of the Spirit is love, joy, peace,
forbearance, kindness, goodness, faithfulness.
GALATIANS 5:22 NIV

I love this verse, Lord! Sandwiched between love and peace we find joy. I pray my child will find joy in that place, too. As he learns to love others, as he experiences peace in his relationships and situations, You bring joy to his heart. I praise You for that. What a huge difference this will make in his life. As he ages, Father, continue to encourage him to be loving and peaceful so that joy will remain with him all his days. Amen.

Exceeding Great Joy

When they saw the star, they rejoiced with exceedingly great joy.
MATTHEW 2:10 KJV

How fun, to think of the wise men seeing the star that guided them to Your Son's birthplace, Father! Locating the King of Kings was cause for great celebration. The same is true in my child's life. When she runs to You, when she discovers You in Your fullness, there is exceedingly great joy in her heart. . .and mine! In Yours, too! May she never tire of following after You. Amen.

Heart-Song

I will shout for joy and sing your praises,
for you have ransomed me.
PSALM 71:23 NLT

Sometimes we sing with our voices, Lord. Other times You place a song of praise in our hearts that no one else can hear. It's so wonderful to watch my child as he taps his fingers in sync to the internal rhythm You've placed in his heart. As he hums and praises in his own way, my heart is blessed because I know he's hearing Your voice, Your melody. What bliss, Lord. Praise You for the privilege of watching him worship. Amen.

A Joyful Princess

After all, what gives us hope and joy,
and what will be our proud reward and crown as we stand before
our Lord Jesus when he returns? It is you!
1 THESSALONIANS 2:19 NLT

I've watched my daughter play "princess" so many times, Father. It always makes me smile because I know that she really is one. She's Your daughter, after all. As wonderful as it is to watch her role-play, I know a greater day is coming. As Your daughter, she will stand in Your presence when You return. Her walk with You will be rewarded, and the crown will be very real, not made out of plastic and plastic jewels. What joy that day will be. . .for all of us! Amen.

Splashing Over. . .Joy!

And these things write we unto you, that your joy may be full.
1 JOHN 1:4 KJV

Father, I pray for overflowing joy in my child's life today. Fill him to the point where it runs over, like a water glass spilling over and running down the sides. Fill him from the inside out so that he will spill out onto others, touching them with contagious joy that comes straight from Your heart. Even if he's facing obstacles—*especially* if he's facing obstacles—fill him so that he may be empowered from within. With such an abundance of supernatural joy, many lives will be touched. Many hearts will be healed, and before long, they're touched, too. So, let it flow! Amen.

A Treasure Chest of Joy

The kingdom of heaven is like treasure hidden in a field.
When a man found it, he hid it again, and then in his
joy went and sold all he had and bought that field.
MATTHEW 13:44 NIV

Father, today I pray that my child would experience the kind of joy that comes when one finds a hidden treasure. May he know what it's like to know You, not just in word or deed, but deep in his heart. May he feel as if he's stumbled across a rare treasure—one so priceless he would be willing to trade everything he owned to have it. May he give his heart to You fully, completely, wholly. May he accept Your work on Calvary and experience new life. Oh, what immeasurable joy will come to our whole family, knowing our child has placed that treasure in his heart for all eternity! Amen.

A Joyful Noise

Make a joyful noise unto the LORD, all ye lands.
PSALM 100:1 KJV

Father, it's not always easy to be vocal with our praise. Yet Your Word is clear! If we truly follow the pattern of Old Testament saints, we will repeatedly lift our voices in thanksgiving! We will let others know. I know that my child is learning from my example, so I pray You give me the courage to speak up. To sing. To praise. To offer joyful thanks to the Lord in such a way that my child will watch and learn. May this joy rise up and overflow in such a way that I can't contain myself. When it spills over, may it spill over onto my child so that she, too, can learn what it means to make a joyful noise. Amen!

Attitude Equals Outcome

Serve the LORD with gladness:
come before His presence with singing.
PSALM 100:2 KJV

Attitude is everything. Our attitude determines our outcome. We've heard this all of our lives, Lord. I know that we are challenged by scripture to serve with gladness. Please help me to demonstrate this to my child, who doesn't always equate service with joy. He's not keen on cleaning up after himself and certainly doesn't celebrate when I ask him to do chores around the house. Yet I've learned one thing from experience: If we serve with an attitude of joy, it changes everything. Our "service" doesn't feel like "service" anymore. It's a privilege! Amen.

Bubbling Joy

Can both fresh water and salt water flow from the same spring?
JAMES 3:11 NIV

All kids love to play with bubbles, Lord, even the big kids! Today my prayer is that my child will experience the "bubbling up" kind of joy that only You can bring. It's such a supernatural thing, kind of like adding water to liquid soap. The result is something mesmerizing. I pray my child feels that bubbling in her belly and can sense it rising to the surface. Your joy—the kind we learn about in Your Word—comes from the deepest place inside of us, so deep that we often forget it's there at all. It rises up, up, up to the surface and the most delightful thing happens. That's what I want for my child. May Your joy squelch any negative emotions she is facing. Let the bubbling begin! Amen!

A Life of Joy

These things we write, so that our joy may be made complete.
1 JOHN 1:4 NASB

Lord, I've discovered the perfect recipe for joy—spending my days loving on others, bringing a smile to their faces. I pray my child learns this recipe for happiness, as well. When he shifts his focus from himself to others, he accomplishes two things: he will spread joy while satisfying his own soul. May his joy be complete in You, wholly focused on what makes Your heart happy, not what makes his own happy. For in that place, sandwiched between You and him, are all of the friends and loved ones whose lives he can affect. May his joy spill over onto them today, Lord. Amen.

Joy in the Family

Now the God of hope fill you with all joy and peace in believing,
that ye may abound in hope, through the power of the Holy Ghost.
ROMANS 15:13 KJV

Father, I know from personal experience that living in a family environment isn't always easy. Brothers and sisters argue. Tempers flare. People (sometimes even Mom and Dad) get their feelings hurt. Yet when we come to You and ask for Your joy, You can (and do) overcome those obstacles. Thank You for teaching me this (sometimes hard) lesson, and thank You for caring enough about my child to spread that lesson even further. May Your joy bind our family together and give us peace and hope in every situation. Amen!

Gladness and Joy

And in every province and in every city, wherever the king's
command and his edict reached, there was gladness
and joy among the Jews, a feast and a holiday.
ESTHER 8:17 ESV

Whole people groups can be affected by joy at one time, can't they, Lord? It's interesting to think about, but it's true. When Your commands and edicts are heeded, my whole family is changed. My children get to experience that with me. With change, comes joy. When we're joyously changed, we affect our neighbors. Then they experience change, resulting in a more joyous household. Then, with like-minded neighbors, we affect our community, and our community affects the world. Joy is like a little ember that spreads into a wildfire. May that fire never go out, Father! Amen.

CHAPTER FOUR

Friffyndships

Friendship is vital to all of us. No matter our age, we love to be surrounded by people who "get" us, people who want to stick around, even when we mess up. Our children are surrounded on every side when they're at school, at church, at play . . .but not necessarily by the kids we would've chosen. That's why it's so important to pray every day for godly friendships for our impressionable kiddos.

Where do we start? How do we pray for godly friendships for our kids? It starts in our own lives. We need to surround ourselves with like-minded people who will lift us up, not pull us down. Our children will observe our friendships and learn by example.

Friendship works both ways: we have to be a friend to have a friend. As grownups, we understand this. Our children are on a learning curve. They often wonder why they're friendless, or why they're not as popular as the other kids. Teaching them how to be a true friend is so important.

Of course, Jesus was the very best teacher. He led the disciples and taught by example—loving people, caring for their needs, and going out of His way to ensure their comfort and well-being. A true friend has compassion. A true friend forgives. A true friend doesn't get hung up on bitterness or jealousy. A true friend lays down his life (goes the extra mile) even when it hurts.

Before we can teach our children to be great friends, we

have to master the art of friendship ourselves. It's never too late to learn. Maybe it's time to step away from a few unproductive, negative relationships and focus on the ones that build us up. Maybe it's time to love deeper, share more, and draw closer to the ones who really matter. In doing so, we won't just build our own relationships; we'll be teaching our children to do the same.

If you're struggling to know how to "teach" friendship skills to your child, remember: God is the very best friend we will ever have. Look to His example. Check out the stories in the Bible where He befriended His people and gave of Himself or them. Talk about an example we can glean from! We can't give up if our child's friends aren't perfect. News flash: our children aren't, either. They're growing, of course, and that's what's important. A "perfect" friend? There's really only one of those, and He gave the ultimate sacrifice, laying down His life on the cross for all of those He called "friend."

It's time to pray, parents. Let's go to the Lord and ask Him to build godly friendships that will stand the test of time.

Closer Than a Brother

One who has unreliable friends soon comes to ruin,
but there is a friend who sticks closer than a brother.
PROVERBS 18:24 NIV

Ah, friends! How we love them, Lord! I'm so grateful for the friends in my own life and pray that you send exactly the right friends for my child, as well. May she come to experience "real" friendship (the "sticks closer than a brother" kind). Being surrounded by lots of so-called friends is okay, but having a true friend, one who won't leave her when she's down or hurting, is even better. Do You have someone special in mind, Father? If so, unite their hearts and bond them. Be in the very center of their relationship, Lord, so that they never stray from You as a dynamic duo. Amen!

Walking with the Wise

Walk with the wise and become wise,
for a companion of fools suffers harm.
PROVERBS 13:20 NIV

I know what it's like to walk with fools, Lord. I've been down that road, swept in by their chatter and easily swayed to link arms when I should've run the other way. When it comes to my child, I pray for the right kind of companions. Not the foolish ones. Not the ones who work overtime to sway others. I want the kind of friends for my child who will help him grow in wisdom. The kind who will be bold enough to say "No way! You're not going to do that!" when needed. Please give me wisdom and discernment where my child's friends are concerned. I don't want to be manipulated or swayed by the pretenders. Amen.

Cautious in Friendship

*The godly give good advice to their friends;
the wicked lead them astray.*
PROVERBS 12:26 NLT

Ah, caution! The yellow light. How we need it, Lord! I need it in so many areas of my life and my child needs it in her life, too. The yellow light warns us when something's not right. When the person we're hanging out with isn't good for us. When we're about to get into trouble. The yellow light says, "Slow down! You're headed for disaster!" It usually preempts a red light, a complete stop. Father, I don't want my child to come to a complete halt in her friendships, but I do pray that You would caution her if she's headed into the danger zone. Flash that light bright, Lord, and may she respond with caution. Amen.

Power in Numbers

*Two are better than one, because they have a good return for
their labor: If either of them falls down, one can help the other up.
But pity anyone who falls and has no one to help them up.*
ECCLESIASTES 4:9–10 NIV

Father, I know there is power in numbers. When we gather together with like-minded people, You are there in the midst. I'm reminded of that today as I think about my child's circle of friends. May she be surrounded on every side by people who can lift her up, bring encouragement, and give her the courage to put one foot in front of the other, even when she's scared. May she be a blessing to her friends, as well. When they all work together, they can do amazing things, Lord! Thank You for binding her heart to godly friends. Amen.

Rocky Places

If anyone has caused grief, he has not so much grieved me as he has grieved
all of you to some extent—not to put it too severely. The punishment inflicted
on him by the majority is sufficient. Now instead, you ought to forgive and
comfort him, so that he will not be overwhelmed by excessive sorrow.
I urge you, therefore, to reaffirm your love for him.
2 Corinthians 2:5–8 niv

We've all been through rocky places in friendships, Father. We hit bumpy roads. Feelings get hurt. Awesome, godly friends separate—part ways—because of foolish things. I pray that my child would be protected from such foolish divisions. Give him the courage to ask for forgiveness when the need arises, and give him just as much courage to extend forgiveness when others have hurt him. I pray that his friendships would be healthy, healed and whole, and run the gamut of time. The enemy is working overtime to separate good friends, Father. I pray for unity and healing, not just for my child, but in my relationships, as well. Amen.

Friendship at First Sight

After David had finished talking with Saul, he met Jonathan, the king's son.
There was an immediate bond between them, for Jonathan loved David.
From that day on Saul kept David with him and wouldn't let him return home.
And Jonathan made a solemn pact with David,
because he loved him as he loved himself.
1 Samuel 18:1–3 nlt

Lord, thank You for bonding me with godly friends! Many of my friendships have lasted for years. Will You do me a favor, Father? Give my child those same long-lasting friendships. I pray he finds godly "bond at first sight" friends in the same way that David found his BFF, Jonathan. These sorts of friends naturally gravitate to one another. They "get" each another. They laugh together, play together, study together, and go through tough times together. They experience ups and downs, but always stick together. Thank You for sending my child "friendship at first sight" friends. Amen.

The Trouble with Gossip

A troublemaker plants seeds of strife;
gossip separates the best of friends.
PROVERBS 16:28 NLT

Gossip is such a problem at every age. I've found myself caught up in it many times over, Lord, and I know my child struggles with this, too. Gossip divides. It causes pain. It's often exaggerated or rooted in a lie. I pray that my child only speaks the truth. May she be drawn to truth-telling friends, as well. Guard her words so that they uplift and encourage, not tear down and wound. When she does go through seasons where gossip is involved, please heal all of the broken places and bind up any wounds so that her friendships can be strong. Thank You for having such a loving heart for her, Lord! Amen.

The Friendship Guide

One who is righteous is a guide to his neighbor,
but the way of the wicked leads them astray.
PROVERBS 12:26 ESV

It's interesting to think of friends as guides, Lord, but that's just what they are. They either guide us down the right path or the wrong path. Today I ask that You give my child great guides. May she link arms with friends who are following Your Word, Your ways. May she naturally be drawn to those who take steps in the right direction. May she learn to be a great guide, as well. . .stepping out in faith and leading by example. No off-course walking, Lord! May her feet be firmly established. Amen.

Building Up

Let no corrupting talk come out of your mouths, but only such as is good for building up, as fits the occasion, that it may give grace to those who hear. And do not grieve the Holy Spirit of God, by whom you were sealed for the day of redemption. Let all bitterness and wrath and anger and clamor and slander be put away from you, along with all malice. Be kind to one another, tenderhearted, forgiving one another, as God in Christ forgave you.
EPHESIANS 4:29–32 ESV

Father, today I ask that You teach my child how to be a godly friend. Guard his mouth, Lord. May he speak words that build up, not tear down. Guard his heart, that he won't be angry. May he be kindhearted toward others. Guard his memories, so that he won't hang on to bitterness. May he learn to extend forgiveness. All these things I pray. Amen.

Iron Sharpens Iron

Iron sharpens iron, and one man sharpens another.
PROVERBS 27:17 ESV

Father, I know the benefit of having friends who "sharpen" me. Where I am strong, they are weak. Where they are weak, I am strong. We are a great team because we're constantly sharpening each other. Today, would You give my child friends who can sharpen her? Can You give her someone she trusts enough to listen to godly advice? I know that "sharpening" isn't always pleasant, but with the right friends it's less painful. Thank You for placing "sharpeners" in her life. Amen.

Wise and Strong

A wise man is full of strength,
and a man of knowledge enhances his might.
PROVERBS 24:5 ESV

My child is always talking about how strong he is, Lord. He's convinced he's super-human, like the characters he sees on TV and in movies. He wants to scale walls, fly through the air, and lift obstacles. Today I'm reminded that the one thing he needs above all others, in order to truly be strong, is wisdom. When he's wise, he's filled with strength. This is especially true in his friendships. May he choose wisely, Lord, so that (together) they can be strong and mighty. Amen.

———

Where You Go, I Will Go

But Ruth said, "Do not urge me to leave you or to return from following you.
For where you go I will go, and where you lodge I will lodge.
Your people shall be my people, and your God my God. Where you die I will die,
and there will I be buried. May the LORD do so to me and more also if
anything but death parts me from you."
RUTH 1:16–17 ESV

Oh, Lord! I want this kind of friendship for my daughter. May she (like Ruth) find someone of whom she can say, "Please don't ask me to leave you. I want to hang out with you, stick with you, and go through thick and thin with you. Grow up with you. Learn from you. Teach you." May she be that kind of friend for others, Father, I pray. Amen.

So Sweet!

Oil and perfume make the heart glad,
and the sweetness of a friend comes from his earnest counsel.
PROVERBS 27:9 ESV

There's something sweet-smelling about a godly friendship, Lord. There's no stinky after-aroma when you're hanging out with someone who's like-minded and pure. That's what I desire for my daughter. I want her to have sweet friends, friends who leave a pleasant aroma, even after they part ways. I want that sweetness to linger as they grow close, as they giggle and laugh over the little things. Most of all, I pray for sweet, quiet moments of conversation between them, where godly counsel flows. What a blessing such a friend can be! Please give her that kind of friend today, I pray. Amen.

Temper, Temper!

Make no friendship with a man given to anger, nor go with a wrathful man, lest you learn his ways and entangle yourself in a snare. Be not one of those who give pledges, who put up security for debts. If you have nothing with which to pay, why should your bed be taken from under you?
PROVERBS 22:24–27 ESV

We all know what it's like to have temperamental friends. I've had a few myself, Lord. They can be scary at times; especially the ones who tend to blow up at every little thing. My prayer for my child is that he would have "temperate" (emotionally healthy) friends, not friends with tempers. There's enough anger in this world without my child having to be subjected to this in his relationships. So, please give him discernment. May he choose wisely. Amen!

CHAPTER FIVE

Dreams and Goals

M ost of us had grandiose dreams when we were young. We wanted to be all sorts of things when we grew up: doctors, teachers, pilots, firefighters, astronauts, Olympic athletes, president of the United States, and so on. We dreamed of all the things we would accomplish and set our sights on the various goals, never thinking or worrying about the obstacles. Today's children are no different. In fact they're probably bigger dreamers than we were. The superhero mentality abounds!

The truth is: few people grow up to be who they thought they would be. Most don't travel to the moon or go to the Olympics. Very few become millionaires or presidents. In fact, most end up working rather "ordinary" jobs. Does this mean their dreams haven't come true? Not at all! In fact, most adults would say that their grown-up version of success is vastly different from the childhood version.

So, how do we pray for our children as they dream of who they one day will be? Do we pray that all of their dreams come true, or pray for wisdom and clarity to know which dreams to follow after? Do we encourage them to try anything and everything, or limit their possibilities to a more realistic number? If we're not careful, we'll end up over our heads, driving to soccer practice, ballet class, piano lessons, swim team, ice skating lessons, karate class, and so on. It can become overwhelming!

Each child is different, of course, and each parent will respond accordingly. If your child is a big dreamer (sees himself doing huge things when he's grown), you'll need to walk a fine line of encouraging while adding doses of reality checks along the way. You'll need to amp up your prayer life, giving God full reign.

Just remember one very important thing: your child is created in the image of a very creative Creator! He's a big dreamer because that's the way God created him. We don't want to crush his dreams. There's nothing worse than seeing a child's hopes and dreams splattered. So, use caution, parents. Be realistic. (There are only so many years of private lessons you can afford, anyway.) Don't blow out the candle of hope. Give those kiddos a reason to think they will do something grand and glorious when they're grown. They will. If they walk with the Lord all of their lives, they will fulfill the most important goal ever set for them.

Let's get busy praying about that, shall we? Those little dreamers need our covering!

Created By a Creator

The plans of the diligent lead surely to abundance,
but everyone who is hasty comes only to poverty.
PROVERBS 21:5 ESV

You are such a creative God! You spun the world into existence with just a word. I know You created us to be creative, too. That's why You're so interested in our dreams and goals. You planted them in our hearts. Today I ask You to stir up my child's dreams. Give him goals, then follow that up with motivation, I pray. May he never lose sight of the fact that he's created in Your image and You are a creative God. May his God-breathed dreams come to fruition in his life, I pray. Amen.

———

Tucking Away the Disappointments

Brothers, I do not consider that I have made it my own.
But one thing I do: forgetting what lies behind and straining
forward to what lies ahead, I press on toward the goal for
the prize of the upward call of God in Christ Jesus.
PHILIPPIANS 3:13–14 ESV

Father, it's sometimes hard to watch my child live with yesterday's disappointments instead of today's possibilities. I pray that You renew her mind, Lord. Help her forget the things that didn't work out and cause her to dream again. Hope again. Set her sights on things above so that she can see her future as hopeful, shiny, filled with possibilities. Remind her that dreams and goals are a good thing and that yesterday's mess-ups won't stop tomorrow's step-ups. You're such a good God! Thank You for keeping my daughter focused. Amen.

Patience, Dreamer!

"But you, take courage! Do not let your hands
be weak, for your work shall be rewarded."
2 CHRONICLES 15:7 ESV

It's so easy to give up when things don't happen overnight, Lord. I've experienced this myself. You help us give birth to dreams and we step out in faith. Yet when things don't happen immediately, we tend to give up. Sometimes we even forget. When it comes to my children, I pray this doesn't happen, Father. Give them God-sized dreams, things they can't accomplish on their own. When those dreams don't come true right away, give them the one thing that's even more important than the dream itself: faith. Their work (and patience) will be rewarded as You lead them on this. Amen!

Make It Plain

And the LORD answered me: "Write the vision; make it plain on tablets,
so he may run who reads it. For still the vision awaits its appointed time;
it hastens to the end—it will not lie. If it seems slow, wait for it;
it will surely come; it will not delay."
HABAKKUK 2:2–3 ESV

Father, we all long to hear Your voice. This is true in my own life and my child's, as well. When we're hearing You clearly, Your direction is just as clear. That's my prayer for my child. May He hear so clearly that Your words seem like second nature to him. When it comes to his hopes and dreams—rather, Your hopes and dreams for his life—please make it plain, Father. Leave no room for doubt. What comfort he will find as he rests in the assurance of Your Word! Amen.

Delighted in Him!

Delight yourself in the LORD,
and he will give you the desires of your heart.
PSALM 37:4 ESV

I remember how fun it was to be young, Lord. I delighted in so many things. The future seemed so bright and cheerful. I love this scripture because it's a reminder, not just to my child, but to me, as well. When we delight ourselves in You, You give us the desires of our heart. How easy it is to forget that. May my child continue the "delights of youth" all of her days, even when she's my age. With that delight comes great joy. Bless You for reminding me today! Amen.

Press On!

I press on toward the goal for the prize
of the upward call of God in Christ Jesus.
PHILIPPIANS 3:14 ESV

To win the prize, we have to keep pressing on. Pressing on is hard work, though, and my kiddo doesn't always feel like working hard, Lord. Remind him today that he was created to do great things for You. Enlarge his vision. Remind him of the prize of the upward call. Then help that sweet boy take the first step. And the second. And the third. Pick him up when he falls (which he surely will), brush him off, and put him back on the road again. Don't let him give up, Father. Encourage him to keep pressing on. Amen.

Building Your House

Prepare your work outside; get everything ready for
yourself in the field, and after that build your house.
PROVERBS 24:27 ESV

It's one thing to dream, another thing to work hard to see your dreams come true. Lord, I'm convinced You're the one who places inspired dreams and goals in our hearts, and I know You long to see them fulfilled and know ahead of time just how much work it's going to take. Please give my children the tenacity they need not only to dream, but to work, work, work to see their dreams come to pass. Anything worth having is worth working for. You know that and I know that. My children? They're on a learning curve! Inspire them, Lord, I pray. Amen.

Count the Cost

For which of you, desiring to build a tower, does not first sit
down and count the cost, whether he has enough to complete it?
LUKE 14:28 ESV

Sometimes our dreams are carefully thought out, Lord, and sometimes we dive in without thinking or praying to make sure You're behind them! I've watched my child come up with ideas that felt right in the moment, but turned out to be bad in the long run. Sometimes the sacrifice is greater than the good. If the cost is too high, if she's in over her head, then please show me how I can reel her back in, Father. I want her to dream, but need to make sure she's prepared to handle the consequences when she moves forward. Thank You for guiding both of us! Amen.

Straight Paths

*Trust in the LORD with all your heart, and do not lean on
your own understanding. In all your ways acknowledge him,
and he will make straight your paths.*
PROVERBS 3:5–6 ESV

My child faces so many crooked roads, Father. She ping pongs from
project to project, friend to friend. One minute she's interested in
ballet, the next she wants to take singing lessons. One minute she
wants to perform on the stage, the next she's asking to be signed up
for soccer. With so many possibilities in front of her, she's truly feeling
her way, waiting for the right path. I'm enjoying this journey with her,
Lord, because I know that I can trust You to make all of the crooked
paths straight. Thank You for that assurance, Father! Amen.

All Things

I can do all things through him who strengthens me.
PHILIPPIANS 4:13 ESV

I know my children so well, Lord, and know when they're struggling. I
wonder sometimes if they realize how powerful You are, and how much
You long to prove that in their lives. As they make their plans—grand
and glorious as they are—won't You sweep in and prove Your power?
Show up in a big way, Father. Surprise them with strength. Arm them
for the tasks they have to face. More than anything, draw them to You
so that they can learn, once and for all, where true strength comes
from. Amen.

Hearing with Clarity

*Do not be conformed to this world, but be transformed by the
renewal of your mind, that by testing you may discern what is
the will of God, what is good and acceptable and perfect.*
ROMANS 12:2 ESV

Discerning Your will can be tricky at times, Lord. With so many voices
crowding in around me, it's sometimes hard to tell which one is Yours.
That's why I'm coming to You today, asking that You speak clearly,
not just to me, but to my child. When she hears Your voice with clarity, she moves with confidence. When she understands what is "good,
acceptable, and perfect" (by Your standards, not the world's) she's able
to make better choices and step out on the things You tell her to do.
Thank You, Father, that You're conforming my child into Your image!
Amen.

To Do His Will

*Jesus said to them, "My food is to do the will
of him who sent me and to accomplish his work."*
JOHN 4:34 ESV

Reading the words "to do the will of Him who sent me" gives me
chills, Father! If Your Son, Jesus, lived to do Your will, how critical
it is for us, Your kids, to do the same. As a parent, I long to do Your
will. I long for my children to catch the vision of "doing the will of
Him who sent them" as well. With so many plans in the works, so
many things stirring in their young lives, they need to know Your will
in every situation. More than that, they need to know that living an
obedient life—desiring to please You by "doing" Your will, is one of
the greatest pleasures they will ever know. Thank You, Father. Amen.

An Enlarged Vision

"Enlarge the place of your tent, and let the curtains of
your habitations be stretched out; do not hold back;
lengthen your cords and strengthen your stakes."
ISAIAH 54:2 ESV

Lord, my children have a tendency to live within the boundaries they've come to know. I can't imagine them "living large," but I know You can. You have huge dreams for them. My prayer for them today is that the curtains of the habitations be stretched out. Begin to prepare them for great and awesome things, Father. As this verse says, don't hold back! What an amazing thought. . .my children could actually make an impact in this world. So, enlarge their dwelling places. Take them beyond what they know and into new ideas, new projects, and new opportunities. I can't wait to see what the future holds. Bless You, Lord! Amen.

Established

In their hearts humans plan their course,
but the LORD establishes their steps.
PROVERBS 16:9 NIV

We get so excited about where we're going sometimes, Lord. We jump out and run toward the goal. Sometimes we get ahead of You. I've seen my child do this. It's likely that he learned it from me. It's good to know Your Word says that we can make plans, but You're the one who establishes our steps. When we move in the wrong direction, You reel us back in. When we're sprinting too fast, You slow us down. Thank You for establishing my child's steps, Father. I know I can trust You to guide him every step of the way. Amen.

CHAPTER SIX

Salt and Light

The Lord calls us to be salt and light, no matter our age. We take this call very seriously. Reaching out to others—sharing the Gospel—isn't always easy, but it's something we're all called to do. We have quite a mission field, don't we! The world is desperate for the Gospel message.

Sometimes we forget that our children have a mission field, too. We're so focused on getting them through school, making good grades, and keeping their room clean, that we overlook their saltiness. We forget to encourage them to reach out to their peers and to shine their lights.

If we pause to think about all of the scriptures about children (particularly the instances where Jesus calls the children to gather around him) we will surely realize how much God values them in His Kingdom. In fact, He says the kingdom of heaven is like a child. If He places this much value on our child's role in kingdom-things, we should, as well!

Children have the power to change the world. Most don't have a lot of inhibitions. They're not yet at the "Please don't make me do that" stage when they're young. They're bolder than we are at times, and more likely to speak their minds. (Boy, isn't that the truth!)

So, how can you pray for your child to be an effective witness? Think about those he comes in contact with: friends, teachers, the kids on the bus, and the not-so-nice kids on the playground. This is his mission field. His work on that field is just as important as yours. Pray that he begins to see others as God's kids, even when they don't exhibit godly attributes.

While you're praying, why not come up with outreach ideas for your family. Perhaps you can volunteer at a homeless shelter. Raise funds for a missionary. Take a short-term missions trip. Provide Christmas gifts for a needy family. Maybe you can make meals for a shut-in or provide school supplies for a child who can't afford them.

There are so many ways to minister to others, and many of those ways are so simple we overlook them. Begin to think salty thoughts. In doing so, you'll spill over onto your child. Before long, you'll be the saltiest family on the block, with lights so bright the neighbors will wonder what they're looking at.

Let's get busy praying. It's time to infuse our kiddos with some salt and light.

Go!

"Therefore go and make disciples of all nations, baptizing them in the name of the Father and of the Son and of the Holy Spirit, and teaching them to obey everything I have commanded you. And surely I am with you always, to the very end of the age."
MATTHEW 28:19–20 NIV

It's hard to think about my children leaving home one day, Father. It makes my heart a little sad to know that my nest will empty and they will step out into the world to make a difference among their peers. Your Word calls us to go into all the world. You want my child to be salt and light now, in his school, his relationships, and his work ethic. You want my child to one day step out of this cozy nest I've created to impact the world in a major way. Start spreading that salt now, I pray. May he be a light to all he sees. Amen.

Whoever Believes

For God so loved the world that he gave his one and only Son, that whoever believes in him shall not perish but have eternal life.
JOHN 3:16 NIV

I'm not crazy about all of my child's friends, Father. I admit it. Some of them rub me the wrong way. It's not that they're bad kids. They're just. . .different. They have different habits, different upbringings, and different ways of communicating. While they might not always be easy to love, I'm reminded in Your Word that You adore them, even the quirkiest ones. In fact, You love them so much that You sent Your Son to save them all. Remind me when those kids are in my home of Your great love for them, I pray. Amen.

Light to All

Neither do people light a lamp and put it under a bowl.
Instead they put it on its stand, and it gives light to everyone in the house.
MATTHEW 5:15 NIV

Sometimes we pick and choose whom we want to share the Good News with, Lord. We get irritated with people and we think they wouldn't want to hear it. We judge them by external appearance or attitude and assume they would be the last person in the world who would ever want to hear. Our kids are learning from us. They begin to pick and choose who they share the Gospel with, too, and often based on similar prejudices. Soften our hearts, Father. Show us (both of us) whom to reach. May we see those people as You see them, worthy of Your life and of eternal life. Amen.

His Witnesses

"You are my witnesses," declares the LORD, "and my servant whom I have chosen, that you may know and believe me and understand that I am he. Before me no god was formed, nor shall there be any after me."
ISAIAH 43:10 ESV

Hearing the word *witness* makes me think of a courtroom, Lord. I don't like the idea of having to take the witness stand. It's scary! What the witness says could change someone else's outcome. Sometimes I feel that way when it comes to witnessing to others about Your love and Your grace, too. I'm scared to speak up, afraid I'll get it wrong or do more harm than good. I'm afraid my child is learning to be a timid witness, based on how she sees me communicate with others. Would You give me courage so that she can be brave, too? Thank You, Lord. Amen.

Can't Hold Back!

*"For we cannot but speak of what
we have seen and heard."*
ACTS 4:20 ESV

I love watching my child get excited, Lord. He talks a mile a minute. Sometimes I have to ask him to slow down so that I can make sense of it all. That's how it is when we've fallen head over heels into a relationship with You. We can't hold back. We want to rush to people to tell them the good news. Today I pray that You would give my child this kind of enthusiasm, not conjured up, but very, very real. The genuineness will be convincing as he shares with his peers. Thank You for that! Amen.

Sharing What We've Witnessed

*For you will be a witness for him to
everyone of what you have seen and heard.*
ACTS 22:15 ESV

It's one thing to hear good news; it's another thing to see it for ourselves, Lord. When we witness something remarkable, we're stunned . . .and excited to share. The story is so remarkable that we can't help but share. Father, I thank You for moving in a remarkable way in my child's life so that she has stories to tell about the things You've done. The miracles. The graces. The open doors. May she not forget even one of the things You've done for her, and may she share, share, share, so that others will be won to You by her testimony. Amen.

Power to Witness

*"But you will receive power when the Holy Spirit has come upon you;
and you shall be My witnesses both in Jerusalem, and in all Judea
and Samaria, and even to the remotest part of the earth."*
ACTS 1:8 NASB

Father, as I read this verse I'm reminded of Popeye the sailor man. Before he ate his spinach, he was a weakling. Afterward, he could conquer any foe! Today I pray that my child will receive the kind of power spoken about in this verse—straight from the Holy Spirit. I can picture him now, like Popeye, going from weak to strong as he learns to trust in You. Once his strength grows, he will have power to witness to others as never before. I'm looking forward to that day, Father! Amen.

Not Ashamed

*For I am not ashamed of the gospel, for it is the power of God for salvation
to everyone who believes, to the Jew first and also to the Greek.*
ROMANS 1:16 NASB

We've all suffered from feelings of shame at some point in our lives, Lord. Whether we're ashamed of how we grew up or ashamed of the clothing we had to wear. . .we all know what it's like to waver in our confidence. Today I pray for my child, that she would never be ashamed of Your Gospel. May she always talk about You with confidence. No shame over living a pure life. No shame over being different from peers. No shame over taking a strong stand for holiness. Thank You, Father, that her passion for the Gospel outweighs any shame. Amen.

Giving an Answer

But sanctify the Lord God in your hearts: and be ready always
to give an answer to every man that asketh you a reason
of the hope that is in you with meekness and fear.
1 PETER 3:15 KJV

It's one thing to have faith in You, Lord. . .another to have to give an answer for that faith. I know from personal experience that explaining my beliefs to others isn't always easy, especially the people who seem to want to confront me. When it comes to my children, I pray that they would develop a clear understanding of what they believe, and why. When people ask them about their faith, they won't even flinch. They will always be ready to give an answer because they are secure in You. Thank You, Father! Amen.

Telling. . .and Loving

"By this everyone will know that you are
my disciples, if you love one another."
JOHN 13:35 NIV

Lord, I come to You today with a contrite spirit, ready to admit that I'm sometimes a hypocrite. I say one thing with my mouth—I share the good news of Your Son—and then I lose my cool with someone while I'm driving. I know my children are learning from me. I ask that You show us all how to love others the way You love them. May we not be guilty of sharing the Gospel with our mouths but contradicting it with our lives. Amen.

A Tree of Life

The fruit of the righteous is a tree of life,
and he who wins souls is wise.
PROVERBS 11:30 NIV

I get so excited when I think about the fruit my child is already bearing, Father. It does my heart good when I see growth. Productivity. She's making a difference. The fruit I'm seeing in her life (gifts of the Spirit, godly friendships, and good choices) convinces me that she's making strides. She's growing in her relationship with You and it shows. What a blessing. As she grows, continue to give her opportunities to reach out to others. May her fruit be evident to them, as well. Amen.

Faith Comes by Hearing

Consequently, faith comes from hearing the message,
and the message is heard through the word about Christ.
ROMANS 10:17 NIV

Lord, sometimes we don't listen. At least, I don't. Oh, I pretend to. My child says something to me and I nod or say "Mm-hmm" when I haven't really been paying attention. Thank You for this reminder that faith comes from hearing—really hearing—and that hearing comes through Your Word. I need to hone in, to hear things more clearly, especially Your voice. When my child sees me advancing in this area, she will want to become a better listener, too. May it be so, Lord. Amen.

Visible Works

"In the same way, let your light shine before others,
so that they may see your good works
and give glory to your Father who is in heaven."
MATTHEW 5:16 ESV

Sometimes I see my child doing the sweetest things, Lord. He opens the door for others when we're in public places. He shares his belongings (even his toys or electronics) with his siblings. He bites his tongue when others try to rile him up. He's growing, Father. His light is shining bright. He's not trying to draw attention to himself by doing these things; it's just happening naturally. Thank You for shining through him. Amen.

No Need for Shame

Do your best to present yourself to God as one approved,
a worker who has no need to be ashamed,
rightly handling the word of truth.
2 TIMOTHY 2:15 ESV

We all have things we're ashamed of, Father. I've wanted to pull the covers over my head on more than one occasion and cry out, "Go away! I don't want to be around anyone right now." My child goes through similar seasons. Thank You for drawing her out during times like that, for encouraging her to present herself to You as one who is approved, as a worker who doesn't have anything to be ashamed of. Once shame is washed away, she is free to become all You've called her to be. Bless You for that. Amen.

CHAPTER SEVEN

Fears

———

Let's face it. . .fears abound. We would be lying to ourselves if we said that growing up makes a difference, that fears go away when we're grown. Truth is: we're faced with as many (or more) fears as adults than as children. That's why it's so critical to learn how to confront fears when we're young so that we're not crippled by them when we're older.

Of course, the world is a scary place! All we have to do is turn on the news to see that tragedies abound. We can't even sign in online without getting news flashes. Social media is tough, too. The photos that show up in our news feeds can be traumatizing. With so much stirring around us, we're bound to feel afraid sometimes. In our own lives, we face very real problems, even dangers. Health woes. Job losses. Relationship traumas. . .all of these things threaten to grip us in fear. As believers (and as adults) we're learning how to deal with these fearful seasons. We see things in perspective. We've learned to put our trust in God, who sees all, knows all, and promises never to leave us or forsake us. Knowing He's always there brings reassurance to our hearts.

What about our kids? How do we teach them to live in a scary world without being scared? It starts with the words that come out of our mouths. If we're constantly fretting or worrying, our children will see that we're afraid. It's hard for them to tell if a situation is big or small if we're overreacting to everything. Lest we think they're not paying attention to what we say, think again! They hear the conversations we have with our spouse. They pick up on verbal clues when we're afraid of what's coming around the bend. They know that something is wrong, and it causes fear to wrap itself around their hearts.

Guarding our tongues is key, but it's not just what we say that matters. Our body language speaks volumes! When we're facing real dangers or fears, we might not come out and say "This situation scares me," but we may exhibit behaviors that make it undeniable.

It's time to rethink how we deal with fear, parents. We need to start by praying, not just for our kiddos (how they respond to fearful situations) but for ourselves, too. We are overcomers! Knowing this will make us more confident in our prayer time. Once we really get a glimpse of the role that faith plays, our prayer time will become more of a victorious chant.

Brace yourself, parents. There is a lot of work ahead as you pray for your child to overcome, so let's get to it.

Out, Fear! Out!

There is no fear in love. But perfect love drives out fear,
because fear has to do with punishment.
The one who fears is not made perfect in love.
1 JOHN 4:18 NIV

Father, I know what it's like to be afraid. I'm asking You to please quiet my child's heart today and remove all fear. Wrap Your arms of love around him and remind him that Your perfect love—far greater than mine, even—has the supernatural power to drive out fear, even when facing the scariest obstacles. He can look the toughest problems directly in the eye and speak to them: "Out, fear! Out!" You will respond and fill his heart with courage, Lord. I know You will. Thank You for loving my child enough to supernaturally rid him of his fears today. Amen.

Delivered!

Do not fear the king of Babylon, of whom you are afraid.
Do not fear him, declares the LORD, for I am with you,
to save you and to deliver you from his hand.
JEREMIAH 42:11 ESV

Sometimes my daughter feels stuck, Lord. She wonders if she's going to be able to make it through the challenges she faces. She faces obstacles at school, with her peers, even at church sometimes, that seem insurmountable. I feel bad for her when she's stuck and do what I can to encourage her (build her up and give her courage), but I know the best encouragement comes straight from You. Remind her that she has nothing to be afraid of, even when things look bad. Comfort her heart and give her the courage she needs to overcome, even when things are difficult. Amen.

Courage to Ask for Understanding

But they did not understand what he
meant and were afraid to ask him about it.
MARK 9:32 NIV

When we don't know what to do, Lord, we lean on You. Not always, of course. Sometimes we forget. Sometimes my son forgets, too. Or maybe he's just confused. He's not clear which way to go. He's not always brave enough to ask for Your help because he's not sure he will be able to hear Your voice. Perhaps he's not sure he will understand Your instructions if he does recognize Your voice. Will You work with him on this, Father? Whisper in his ear and help him know You better. Then give him the courage and the direction he needs to face each day as a mighty man of God. Amen.

God Is on Our Side

"Do not be afraid of them, for I am with you
and will rescue you," declares the LORD.
JEREMIAH 1:8 NIV

I've been down that road where I've felt no one was on my side, Lord, so I get it. I know what my child is facing. Sometimes he feels ganged up on. Set apart. Different. Kids aren't always nice. Sometimes adults aren't very nice, either. Yet You, Lord, are loving and kind. Remind my son that You are with him. You are for him. You will rescue him, even when others turn against him. Don't ever let him forget that You're on his side, even when others gang up against him. Knowing this will give him the courage he needs to go far in this life. Praise You for that! Amen!

Holding Hands with God

For I am the LORD, your God, who takes hold of your
right hand and says to you, Do not fear; I will help you.
ISAIAH 41:13 NIV

Lord, what a lovely picture. . .You, taking hold of my right hand! I love it, Lord! Sometimes, when my courage wanes, I feel it, too! Today I'm asking that You take hold of my child's right hand. She needs the reassurance that a loving hand can bring. She needs to let go of her fears, and Your gentle embrace will give her the courage to do that, Father. Give those sweet little fingers of hers a squeeze and remind her that she's never alone. Whisper those words—"Do not fear; I will help you"—into her ear as she faces today's challenges. As she rises up in her spirit to overcome, fear will dissipate, and she will be strengthened from the inside out! Amen.

A Healthy Fear

Fear the LORD, you his holy people,
for those who fear him lack nothing.
PSALM 34:9 NIV

Lord, I know what it is to be afraid, and my child does, too. That's why I'm so grateful that the only kind of fear You recommend is fearing You (treating You with the awe, reverence, and respect You deserve). Today I ask that You replace my child's fear of "things" with a healthy respect and awe for his heavenly Father. Show him that walking hand in hand with You means that he has no reason to be afraid. May he always be mesmerized by Your presence, overwhelmed with awe by the things You've done in his life. Amen.

No Cowering!

For the Spirit God gave us does not make us timid,
but gives us power, love and self-discipline.
2 TIMOTHY 1:7 NIV

Father, I pray that my child will never be the sort to cower in fear, afraid of her own shadow. I don't want her timidity to hold her back, even for a moment. When she's afraid, please comfort her and give her courage to face her fears head-on. May Your love boost her confidence and convince her that she has power and self-discipline when she trusts in You. Thank You for caring about my child, Father. Amen.

What Can Mortal Man Do?

When I am afraid, I put my trust in you. In God, whose word I praise—
in God I trust and am not afraid. What can mere mortals do to me?
PSALM 56:3–4 NIV

Lord, there is no promise in Your Word that we will never be afraid, only that we can trust in You. I love this question in this verse: "What can mortal man do to me?" The answer? "Nothing, as long as I trust in You!" This is a lesson that's taken me years to learn, Father. I'm asking that You speed up the process for my child. Let him know that he can praise his way through any situation and that his enemies (real or imagined) can do him no real harm. He can trust You, Lord. He can rise above his fears. I will do my best to lead by example as I praise my way through my own battles. Together, we'll battle through. Amen.

Hiding Out

He answered, "I heard you in the garden,
and I was afraid because I was naked; so I hid."
GENESIS 3:10 NIV

What an interesting picture, Lord! Adam and Eve in the garden, hiding from You because they were ashamed. I know that "look" in my child's eye when she's ashamed. I know how badly she wants to hide in her room instead of facing me when she's upset or afraid of my reaction to something. I pray that she will never experience that kind of fear when it comes to her relationship with You, Lord. May hiding never be an option or a desire on her part. Instead, I pray she runs to You, even when she's afraid, so that she can experience true peace and joy, even in the toughest of situations. While You're at it, continue to work on me in this area, too! Amen.

Good Decisions

When the men of that place asked him about his wife, he said,
"She is my sister," because he was afraid to say, "She is my wife." He thought,
"The men of this place might kill me on account of Rebekah,
because she is beautiful."
GENESIS 26:7 NIV

I know from experience that fear sometimes causes us to make poor decisions, Lord. I've made a few myself and all because I didn't have the courage to rise up and do the right thing. Throughout time Your people have struggled in this area. (It's obvious from today's scripture that even the "Bible greats" made poor decisions when afraid.) I ask that You give my child the courage he needs to make good decisions today, Lord. May none of his decisions be made out of fear. Amen.

What They Fear

Who is going to harm you if you are eager to do good?
But even if you should suffer for what is right, you are blessed.
"Do not fear what they fear; do not be frightened."
1 PETER 3:13–14 NIV

Father, I'm glad Your Word tells us not to "fear what they fear." They—
the people in this world—are terrified of so many things! Peer pressure. Financial woes. Relationship issues. Current news events. I get it.
There's some scary stuff out there. My family can rise above those fears
with Your help. I ask today that You help our whole family as we stick
together to make a difference in this world. As we seek to "do good"
(bring Your Gospel to those around us) may we not be swallowed up
in fear. Remind my children (and me) every day that sharing the good
news of the Gospel, while frightening at times, is the greatest blessing
of our lives. Amen.

Abba, Father

The Spirit you received does not make you slaves, so that you live in fear
again; rather, the Spirit you received brought about your adoption
to sonship. And by him we cry, "Abba, Father."
ROMANS 8:15 NIV

Thank You for being our Daddy, Lord. Not all of us had great dads.
Today I ask You to make Yourself known as *Abba* ("Daddy") to my
children. Nestle them close to Your heart and make Your presence real
to them. As they draw close, all fears will be washed away from their
hearts. I know this, because it's happened in mine, many times over.
May my children not be slaves to fear. May they come to know the
safety that sticking close to Daddy God can bring. May they walk fear-
free lives, knowing "Abba" will always care for their every need. Amen.

Noble Character

"And now, my daughter, don't be afraid. I will do for you all you ask.
All the people of my town know that you are a woman of noble character."
RUTH 3:11 NIV

It's so hard not to be afraid when our peers can be so forceful and convincing. Peer pressure is such a problem, and not just for my children, Lord! It's even tough as an adult. When I read this scripture from Ruth I'm reminded that being a person of noble character is a good thing, especially when surrounded by peers. When my child is with her friends, they see her for who she is—a believer. A woman of God. They don't always like it, but they know she is a "woman of noble character." Give her the courage to lay down all fears when she's around her peers and be the mighty woman of God You've called her to be. Amen.

Faith

We often ask ourselves, "What is faith?" The Bible answers this question in Hebrews 11:1 (NIV): "Now faith is confidence in what we hope for and assurance about what we do not see." It's hard enough to be confident in what we *do* see; seemingly impossible at times to bolster confidence in the things we can't. That's why we depend on the Lord so much. He gives us the wherewithal to grow our faith—from a tiny mustard seed to something much larger.

Our children are taught to put their faith, their trust, in so many things. Academics. Self. Peers. Talents. Abilities. This is the world's perspective, after all. "Trust in yourself. Believe in yourself." Talk about a skewed message! As parents, we have a difficult task ahead of us, teaching them to place their confidence solely in God. It's a task we're still struggling with ourselves.

So, how do we pray for our children to have an increase in faith? Do we pray for more obstacles that require it? Do we pray for an easy, burden-free life that doesn't require as much faith? Do we pray that they would be surrounded by friends, teachers, and mentors who will instill it by proxy?

We need to pray, as the Bible teaches, for their existing faith to be acted on, even if it's teeny-tiny in size. In other words, we must let them stretch their faith by using it, even in situations that don't seem huge to us. We do this by stopping in the very middle of a situation and praying (out loud) so that our children hear us put our own faith in action. They learn by example to do the same. How wonderful, to watch our prayer lives grow in these individual situations. Before long, those faith-filled "in the moment" prayers will be second nature to our children. They won't wait until nighttime prayers. They won't wait until a designated morning prayer time. They will learn from our example to stop right then, right there, and pray. Doesn't that bring joy to your heart?

As our children grow, so will their faith. Before long we'll be praying for completely different things. When they're teens, we'll pray for their driving abilities. As they fall in love and think about marriage, we'll pray for their spouses-to-be. All of these things will require faith, of course. Look on the bright side: by then, your faith-filled prayers will be second nature.

What are you waiting for, parents? Let's pray the prayer of faith over those kids!

Mustard Seed Faith

He replied, "Because you have so little faith. Truly I tell you,
if you have faith as small as a mustard seed, you can say to this mountain,
'Move from here to there,' and it will move.
Nothing will be impossible for you."
MATTHEW 17:20 NIV

I've often watched my child struggle, Father. It breaks my heart. I wonder how I can help him increase his faith when situations rise up against him. It brings me comfort to realize that You care enough to move on his behalf. Even the teeny-tiniest bit of faith on his part is enough to move the mountains in his life. Show me how to lead by example, speaking to the mountains in my own life, Lord. Amen.

———

Mountain Movers

Jesus replied, "Truly I tell you, if you have faith and do not doubt,
not only can you do what was done to the fig tree, but also you can say
to this mountain, 'Go, throw yourself into the sea,' and it will be done."
MATTHEW 21:21 NIV

Sometimes my child feels invincible, Lord. She speaks with such confidence. Other times, she's afraid of her own shadow. I can't figure her out! I'm asking today that You give her the kind of faith that makes her bold. Remove all doubts from her mind, (not doubts about her own abilities, but Yours). May she never doubt You, Father. May she look at every mountain and see it as You see it, just a pebble in the road. Amen.

Getting Rid of Doubt

Immediately Jesus reached out his hand and caught him.
"You of little faith," he said, "why did you doubt?"
MATTHEW 14:31 NIV

We believe. . .and then we doubt. Doesn't matter our age, Lord; we all do it. Our confidence wanes when we take our eyes off of You and put them on ourselves. Today I ask that You keep my child's focus solely on You and not himself. When doubts creep in (as they so often do) please remind him that the power to change his situation lies in Your hands, not his. Thank You for this reminder in my life, too. Amen.

———

Granted!

Then Jesus said to her, "Woman, you have great faith!
Your request is granted." And her daughter was healed at that moment.
MATTHEW 15:28 NIV

Great faith, Father. . .how we long for it! We don't always feel faith-filled. I know I don't, and I can see in my child's eyes that she struggles in this area sometimes, too. Today I pray that my child will have a supernatural increase of faith. May she have the confidence to approach You—as the woman in this scripture did—and make her requests with the confidence and faith that her request will be granted. Thank You, Father. Amen.

The Shield of Faith

In addition to all this, take up the shield of faith,
with which you can extinguish all the flaming arrows of the evil one.
EPHESIANS 6:16 NIV

I love watching my child play superhero, Father! He's just courageous enough to believe he's got superhuman abilities! With his hand in Yours, he really does have supernatural abilities. When he puts on the shield of faith (far better than any superhero cape) he can—and will—do amazing things for Your kingdom. Show me how to convey this message to him as he grows, Lord, so that he never goes out without that shield. Amen.

Visible Faith

Some men brought to him a paralyzed man, lying on a mat.
When Jesus saw their faith, he said to the man,
"Take heart, son; your sins are forgiven."
MATTHEW 9:2 NIV

I'm amazed by the visible faith that some people have, Lord. They seem to take You at Your word, even in seemingly impossible situations. I want this kind of faith in my own life, Father, and I want it to spill over on my children. When we face really hard things, please remove our doubts and replace them with supernatural faith to believe for impossible things. May we always trust You, no matter how difficult the situation. Amen.

Sure of What We Hope For

Now faith is the substance of things hoped for,
the evidence of things not seen.
HEBREWS 11:1 KJV

It's one thing to be hopeful, another to be absolutely sure that what you're hoping for will actually come true! I know from experience that all of the wishing in the world won't bring things to pass, Lord. Yet faith will. The tiniest little bit of faith will move mountains and change the course of a person's life. That's why I'm asking You to intervene in my child's life and stir up his faith. Make him sure—really, really sure—that You will move on his behalf. Amen.

No Wavering

But let him ask in faith, nothing wavering.
For he that wavereth is like a wave of the sea driven
with the wind and tossed.
JAMES 1:6 KJV

I'm sure You must get tired of our wavering, Lord. Back and forth we go, faith-filled one minute, terrified the next. I'm reminded today that my back-and-forth movement in my spiritual walk is spilling over on my children. I don't want them to follow my lead in this area, Father. I want them to be steady in their faith, not ping-ponging back and forth, as I've sometimes done. Show me how to lead by example, Lord. Steady me. . .so that my children can be steady. Amen.

Creative Faith

By faith we understand that the universe was created by the word of God,
so that what is seen was not made out of things that are visible.
HEBREWS 11:3 ESV

I remember singing the song "He's Got the Whole World in His Hands" as a child, Lord. It's true. . .You do! You created it all by speaking it into existence. What makes us think You're not just as capable of working miracles today? Increase my faith, Lord, so that I can teach my children to pray for miracles, too. Remind us in every situation that You were capable of the miraculous from the very beginning. You won't let us down now. Amen.

Increase!

The apostles said to the Lord, "Increase our faith!"
LUKE 17:5 NASB

It intrigues me, Lord, that even Your own disciples had to ask for an increase of faith. It makes me feel better, to be honest. I'm not alone! If even the ones who walked and talked with Jesus had to ask for more, then I shouldn't feel bad asking—for myself or my child. That's my request today. Grow our family into a faith-filled powerhouse, Father. We ask for increase in every area and anticipate what You're going to do. Amen.

A Man of Faith

The statement found approval with the whole congregation;
and they chose Stephen, a man full of faith.
ACTS 6:5 NASB

I love the story of Stephen, Lord, because I'm reminded that he was chosen—out of a large group of potential candidates—for his faith. You weren't looking for the most talented, the most well-known, or the most sensational. You were looking for a man of faith. My child is a Stephen, Lord. I know You've chosen him to do great things for Your kingdom. I can't wait to see how You use Him, Father! Amen.

Door-Opening Faith

When they had arrived and gathered the church together,
they began to report all things that God had done with them
and how He had opened a door of faith to the Gentiles.
ACTS 14:27 NASB

Faith opens doors. I love that image, Lord. It opens doors for people who've made mistakes. It opens doors for people who are weary. It opens doors for young, old, and those in-between. Today I pray for my child. She's facing a few doors. Swing them wide by increasing her faith, Father. May she step through them with confidence in You. Amen.

Act Like a Man

Be watchful, stand firm in the faith,
act like men, be strong.
1 CORINTHIANS 16:13 ESV

How many times have parents spoken the words "Act like a man" to their sons, Lord? Probably thousands, and not always out of kindness. While our boys might not be ready to truly act like grown men, there's something in the imagery of this verse that bolsters faith. What a wonderful scripture: "Act like a man. Be strong. Stand firm in the faith." These are the words I should speak to my child, Lord. No criticism. Just encouragement! May he grow into a mighty man of valor. Amen.

Speak Up!

Since we have the same spirit of faith according to what
has been written, "I believed, and so I spoke," we also believe,
and so we also speak, knowing that he who raised the Lord Jesus
will raise us also with Jesus and bring us with you into his presence.
2 CORINTHIANS 4:13–14 ESV

Lord, there's something about speaking things aloud that reinforces them in our minds. When we speak things, we begin to believe them. Today I would ask that You show my child how to speak words of faith in her everyday life. May she believe (in her heart of hearts) and then boldly speak. May those spoken words touch other lives, as well as her own. Amen.

CHAPTER NINE

Praise Life

———

When we walk closely with the Lord, we can't help but praise Him. It just comes naturally. When He blesses us unexpectedly, we praise. When we view an exquisite pink-and-gold sunset, our hearts want to sing His praise. When we look into the eyes of a newborn baby, we are overcome with gratitude and thanks, as well as awe. Opportunities abound! What about the rough times? Can we—should we—praise then, too? If so, are we doing a good job, so that our children can see and follow our example?

There are so many benefits to praising the Lord. It boosts our confidence. It speaks things into existence. It tears down walls. We can praise our way through any situation. Don't believe it? Consider the story of Jehoshaphat. When he led his people (Israel) into battle against their enemies, he sent the worshippers to the frontlines. Check it out:

> *So they rose early in the morning and went out into the Wilderness of Tekoa; and as they went out, Jehoshaphat stood and said, "Hear me, O Judah and you inhabitants of Jerusalem: Believe in the LORD your God, and you shall be established; believe His prophets, and you shall prosper." And when he had consulted with the people, he appointed those who should sing to the LORD, and who should praise the beauty of holiness, as they went out before the army and were saying: "Praise the LORD, For His mercy endures forever." (2 Chronicles 20:20–21 NKJV).*

Can you imagine being one of the Levites (singers), being sent to the frontlines to worship? Talk about scary. Yet the battle was won as praise led the way.

That's how we want to live, and that's how we want to teach our children to live. Praise can lead the way. It can lead the way when things are going well. It can lead the way when we're struggling to make ends meet. It can lead the way when we have new job opportunities. It can lead the way when we're wondering where the next paycheck is going to come from.

Praise Him as you go about your daily business. Praise Him in the car when you're driving. Your children will find this praise-filled lifestyle very comforting and very tempting. Before long, they'll be singing and praising their way through situations, too.

It's time to praise, parents! God is worthy of our praise!

Giving Thanks

Give thanks to the LORD, for he is good;
his love endures forever.
PSALM 107:1 NIV

Lord, instead of just praying for my child to learn to praise You, I want to start by praising You myself! Thank You, Father, for saving me. Thank You for creating me (and my child) in Your image. I praise You for all of the wonderful gifts You have bestowed upon me, and I praise You, too, for allowing me the privilege of being a parent. I'm learning from You how to be better at that. What an amazing Father You are. You are worthy of praise, Lord! Amen.

A Song of Praise

"The LORD is my strength and song,
and He has become my salvation; This is my God,
and I will praise Him; my father's God, and I will extol Him."
EXODUS 15:2 NASB

Lord, You are my song! You put a song in my heart. Today I pray that my song of worship will spill over onto my child. May she hear my voice lifted in praise. May the words of my mouth be pleasing, not just to You, but to her. May You give me an attitude of praise, even in the hardest of situations, so that she can learn from my example. May she become a "natural" at praising, Father. Fill her heart with Your love song. Amen.

Awesome God!

"Who is like You among the gods, O LORD? Who is like You,
majestic in holiness, awesome in praises, working wonders?"
EXODUS 15:11 NASB

Nothing can compare to You, Father. Absolutely nothing. I stand in awe of You today. Lord, I pray that my child will develop the same sense of wonder and awe as he comes into Your presence. May he see that You are majestic—far more so than any movie character or superhero. May He stand in awe of You as You work in his day-to-day life. You are a wonder-working God, and I'm so grateful for all You're doing in our lives. Amen.

I've Seen It!

"He is your praise and He is your God, who has done these
great and awesome things for you which your eyes have seen."
DEUTERONOMY 10:21 NASB

Lord, there are some things that we just have to see with our own eyes to believe. I've witnessed miracles—people healed, marriages mended, relationships restored. I've seen these things with my own eyes. My prayer for my child today is that You would open her spiritual eyes to see the mighty works You're doing all around her. May she see as never before so that she can respond with praise. May our eyes always be open to Your wonders, Lord! Amen.

Public Praise

*"Hear, O kings; give ear, O rulers! I—to the LORD,
I will sing, I will sing praise to the LORD, the God of Israel."*
JUDGES 5:3 NASB

Father, it's easy to praise You when no one's looking. It's not always so easy in the marketplace of ideas, where people don't see eye to eye. Yet we must lift our voices in praise, especially when we're surrounded by people who doubt Your goodness. I pray today for my child, that he would be willing to speak well of You when surrounded by his peers. May his words about You always be positive and faith-filled, and may the praise inside his heart spill out, no matter where he goes. Amen.

Enemies, Be Gone!

*"I call upon the LORD, who is worthy to be praised,
and I am saved from my enemies."*
2 SAMUEL 22:4 NASB

There are so many benefits to praising You, Lord. Today I'm reminded that my praise sends enemies fleeing. May my child find comfort in this, as well! As she lifts Your name in praise, may her enemies flee. As she continues to worship You, may those who oppose her soften. May their hearts be touched. May their minds be changed. May they find wholeness and healing, so that their lives will be affected. What a difference praise makes! Amen.

Reverent Praise

Worship the LORD with reverence
and rejoice with trembling.
PSALM 2:11 NASB

Lord, sometimes we celebrate our victories, but forget about reverencing You. You are holy, Lord. You're worthy of all of our praise. May I teach my child not just to praise You, but to revere You. May she always know that You are holy. You are awesome. Your deeds are wondrous. May she never lose that sense of awe as she comes into Your presence, Father, and may that awe spill over so that all can see. Amen.

Among the Nations

"Therefore I will give thanks to You, O LORD,
among the nations, and I will sing praises to Your name."
2 SAMUEL 22:50 NASB

Father, You are renowned among the nations. You're not just Lord of my country, my people, my neighborhood, my church. . . You are Lord of all! I pray that You would expand my child's vision to think globally. May he see You as not just "his" God, but "their" God, too. Thank You for the reminder that people all over this great big globe are worshipping You today, Lord—each in their own language and own way. What a beautiful picture that must be! Amen.

Speaking of Wonders

Sing to Him, sing praises to Him;
speak of all His wonders.
1 CHRONICLES 16:9 NASB

We take so many things for granted, Lord. Sometimes we look around at Your creation and forget to be inspired. Forget to be awed. Re-instill a sense of wonder in my child, I pray. May she look around at Your creation—a colorful sunset, a red robin, a field of clover, her baby brother's adorable face—and see You. When she sees You, may her heart burst with song, may her lips speak of Your praises. Amen.

———

Above All

For great is the LORD, and greatly to be praised;
He also is to be feared above all gods.
1 CHRONICLES 16:25 NASB

You are the greatest of the great, Lord. May my child never forget this. You are greater than any teacher he will ever have, any superhero he will ever emulate, any celebrity he will ever admire. Nothing—and no one—will ever come close to You. You are to be revered above all things. My prayer today is that my child will always see You in Your proper place and praise You for who You are. Amen.

Bring an Offering

Ascribe to the LORD the glory due His name; bring an offering,
and come before Him; worship the LORD in holy array.
1 CHRONICLES 16:29 NASB

Praising is so beneficial, but it isn't always easy, Lord. I understand why the Bible often calls it a "sacrifice" of praise. Praise is an offering. It's something we decide to do. I pray that my child will decide to praise, no matter her circumstances. When things are going well, may she praise. When things are tough, may she continue to bring a sacrifice of praise. May she bring her offering—and often. May her sacrifice be a choice, not something she feels she has to do to please me. Amen.

From Everlasting to Everlasting

O give thanks to the LORD, for He is good; for His lovingkindness is
everlasting. Then say, "Save us, O God of our salvation, and gather us and
deliver us from the nations, to give thanks to Your holy name, and glory in
Your praise." Blessed be the LORD, the God of Israel, from everlasting even
to everlasting. Then all the people said, "Amen," and praised the LORD.
1 CHRONICLES 16:34–36 NASB

Lord, it touches my heart to think that my child's generation isn't the first or the last to praise You. From the beginning of time, people across the world have worshipped. Throughout all eternity, Your people will continue to praise. There, in the very middle of it all—my child lifts his heart to praise. What a lovely picture! We praise You, Lord! Amen.

Now

"Now therefore, our God, we thank You,
and praise Your glorious name."
1 CHRONICLES 29:13 NASB

Sometimes we forget to stop in the moment to thank You, Lord. How sad that is! May I teach my child to watch for Your miracles and then respond with praise before another minute goes by. I know he's watching, Father, so help me remember to do this myself. When we're saved from a near-miss accident, may we praise! When we get a good report from the doctor, praise! Even when we face challenges, may I lead by example, offering praise for the miracle yet to come. Amen.

Not to Us

Not to us, O LORD, not to us, but to your name give glory,
for the sake of your steadfast love and your faithfulness!
PSALM 115:1 ESV

We love pats on the back, Lord. I know I do, anyway. I know that my child loves to be encouraged, too. Please help us to remember the "not to us" principle, Father. While encouragement is good (and necessary), the One who's truly worthy of praise is You. May we remember, even with every accomplishment our child makes, to credit You, as well. You're the one who placed those gifts and abilities in him, after all! We praise You, Lord! Amen.

CHAPTER TEN

Bodily Image

Oh, the image in the mirror! We cringe when we're not happy with it. We gripe and complain about all of the things we wish we could change, and then work overtime trying to whip our bodies into shape.

An inappropriate body image can start at any age and can lead to all sorts of problems: depression, eating disorders, even agoraphobia. People who hate the way they look don't want to be around others and will go out of their way to exclude themselves from events. They don't try out for the school play. They don't sing in the choir. They hide away, wishing they could change their appearance so that they would be more loveable. More accepted. We certainly don't want this for our children, though it's a real possibility if they see themselves through a negative filter.

Where does this negative filter come from, and how can we counteract it? Unfortunately, the problem often starts with what they hear from us. We need to guard how we talk about ourselves. Many times we say things like, "I wish I looked different" or "Why can't I get rid of these big hips?" We cut ourselves down, and our children are listening. Instead of seeing ourselves as God sees us, we're self-abasing. This sort of talk has to go.

Another negative filter is television. Actors, actresses, models, TV stars. . .they flood across the screen, their bodies trim, their faces perfectly made up, their clothing exquisite. How can anyone compare? Yet our children often feel they must try.

When they don't measure up (when the image in the mirror doesn't match what they see on TV or in magazines) they get depressed. If they happen to struggle with a few extra pounds or acne, the situation intensifies.

There's really only one way to counteract a negative body image. We have to convince our child to see herself as God sees her, and we must convey the message that she's created in His image. As the old saying goes, "God don't make no junk." His creation is exquisite. He loves every freckle, every mismatched sock, and every imperfect hair. The only "body image" He's concerned with is the body of Christ. . .and we're all members, no matter what we look like.

Dig your heels in deep, parents. Your kiddo needs a lot of prayer to overcome in this area. Pray that she will see herself the way God does, then pray that any insecurities will be washed away as she looks in the mirror and sees—not her own image—but His. Amen?

Wonderfully Made

I praise you because I am fearfully and wonderfully made;
your works are wonderful, I know that full well.
Psalm 139:14 niv

We place too much emphasis on the reflection in the mirror, Lord. This isn't just a problem for our kids; sometimes I struggle with it, too. It breaks my heart to watch my child criticize her appearance. I pray that she will see herself the way You see her. May she have the proper body image. I know that I need to lead by example, Father. May I not put myself down. If I can withhold critique of my own body, perhaps she will learn to do the same. Amen.

A Temple

Or do you not know that your body is a temple of the Holy Spirit
within you, whom you have from God? You are not your own,
for you were bought with a price. So glorify God in your body.
1 Corinthians 6:19–20 esv

My child's body is a temple, Lord. I know that. So I pray that I do the best job I can do as a parent to take care of that little temple for him. Help me to feed him the right foods, make sure he gets proper nutrition and exercise. Help me to share Your thoughts on body image, and help me as I work to convince him that he will one day have to be solely responsible for what he puts into his body. May he see it as the temple it is. Amen.

Look at the Heart

But the LORD said to Samuel, "Do not look on his appearance
or on the height of his stature, because I have rejected him.
For the LORD sees not as man sees: man looks on the outward
appearance, but the LORD looks on the heart."
1 SAMUEL 16:7 ESV

This world seems to judge everything by outward appearance, Father.
It makes me sad. If my child doesn't wear the right shoes, dress in
trendy clothes, or wear her hair in a certain way, then she's looked
down on by her peers. I pray she rises above feelings of inadequacy in
this area and sees herself as the gem she is. On the days when she's not
feeling "pretty", please remind her that she's beautiful to You. Amen.

A Living Sacrifice

I appeal to you therefore, brothers, by the mercies of God,
to present your bodies as a living sacrifice,
holy and acceptable to God, which is your spiritual worship.
ROMANS 12:1 ESV

Lord, we're so hard on our bodies sometimes. We work too hard, sleep
too little, and run ourselves ragged. This is even true of our children.
They face such challenges as balancing schoolwork, sports, and artistic
endeavors. Sometimes I don't do a very good job keeping their schedule in balance. They get tired. Worn down. I forget to present their
little bodies to You as a living sacrifice. Please help me to remember to
do this, Father. Amen.

Vanity

Charm is deceitful, and beauty is vain,
but a woman who fears the LORD is to be praised.
PROVERBS 31:30 ESV

Every girl wants to be pretty, Lord. She wants to look in the mirror and be happy with the face staring back at her. Sometimes girls go too far. They pay too much attention to looking beautiful on the outside and forget about the inside. They pay more attention to outer wardrobe than issues of the heart. Today I pray that my child will see that outward beauty is fleeting. It won't last. A beautiful heart, however? It will last forever. Please show her that, Father. Amen.

Green with Jealousy

Those who belong to Christ Jesus have crucified the flesh with its passions
and desires. If we live by the Spirit, let us also keep in step with the Spirit.
Let us not become conceited, provoking one another, envying one another.
GALATIANS 5:24–26 ESV

I see so many kids who are stuck up, Lord. They're prevalent in my child's circle, and in mine, too. It's a common problem. May my child never put his nose too high in the air. May he not think he's stronger, more handsome, or smarter than any of his peers. May he see himself as You see him, Father—no more and no less. Amen.

Dolled Up

Your beauty should not come from outward adornment,
such as elaborate hairstyles and the wearing of gold jewelry or fine clothes.
1 PETER 3:3 NIV

An "adorned" woman might look beautiful on the outside, but that doesn't always show up in her behavior. We see her poor attitude. The way she treats others. She might be dolled up on the outside, but she's a rag doll on the inside. As I raise my child, I pray that I will be able to instill a different definition of *adorned*. May my child see that the kind of adornment that matters is inward, not outward. There's nothing wrong with being externally dolled up (to some extent, anyway) but a beautiful heart is what matters. Amen.

Walk in His Ways

For we are his workmanship, created in Christ Jesus unto good works,
which God hath before ordained that we should walk in them.
EPHESIANS 2:10 KJV

We fret over bodily image, Father, and sometimes forget about our actions. What good would a pretty face be with an ugly heart? What good would muscular arms be with no spiritual fortitude? What good would a trim physique be with a puffed-up attitude? As I raise my child, Lord, I pray that I can do a good job conveying this truth: we are created in Your image to do good works. It's not about the outer man. It's about the inward one. Amen.

In His Time

He hath made every thing beautiful in his time:
also he hath set the world in their heart, so that no man can find
out the work that God maketh from the beginning to the end.
ECCLESIASTES 3:11 KJV

You're changing my child's body daily, Lord! I see it happening right in front of me. May she not be disappointed with how she looks today, Father. May she see herself—every square inch—as being a work in progress. Your work, Lord. . .is perfect! You won't let her down, Father. Thank You for that promise. Amen.

Stamp of Approval

And God saw every thing that he had made, and, behold,
it was very good. And the evening and the morning were the sixth day.
GENESIS 1:31 KJV

When You looked down on creation, Lord, how You must've smiled. You saw that it was good. You put Your stamp of approval on Your work. Help me teach my child that You've placed Your stamp of approval on him, Lord. In Your sight, he looks very, very good. It's all because of the righteousness of Jesus, Father. My son is beautiful in Your sight because his heart is forever linked to that of Your Son. Praise You! Amen.

I Shall Not Want

The LORD is my shepherd;
I shall not want.
PSALM 23:1 KJV

We want so many things, Father. New shoes. New clothes. Trendy hairstyles. New accessories. We want all of the things that our peers have so that we can fit in. This is true in my child's world, too. So many times he comes to me, asking for things that his friends have, and often so that he can feel loved and accepted by them. Show me how to teach him that You are his shepherd. He doesn't have to chase after his wants and wishes. Amen.

Consider the Lilies

Consider the lilies how they grow: they toil not,
they spin not; and yet I say unto you,
that Solomon in all his glory was not
arrayed like one of these.
LUKE 12:27 KJV

How beautiful Your creation is, Lord! The flower in the field, the changing leaves on the trees. . .exquisite! Your workmanship is breathtaking. We stand in awe as we look at what You've made. These things don't spend time fretting over how they look. The lily doesn't say, "I don't like my appearance today." No way! I pray my child would have the same confidence as she looks in the mirror. She's Your workmanship. May she see herself as such and lay down all insecurities. Amen.

A Heart at Peace

A heart at peace gives life to the body,
but envy rots the bones.
PROVERBS 14:30 NIV

I love Your prescription for good health, Lord! A heart at peace brings life. My child needs to be convinced of this, too. He's not always at peace. He gets frustrated. Envious. He wants what his friends have. According to Your Word, envy is hard on the body. It slows us down. Speak to his heart today, Father. Remind him that he can live a peaceful life, a healthy life, as long as he trusts in You. Amen.

In His Image

Then God said, "Let us make man in our image, after our likeness.
And let them have dominion over the fish of the sea and over the birds of
the heavens and over the livestock and over all the earth and over every
creeping thing that creeps on the earth." So God created man in his own
image, in the image of God he created him; male and female he created them.
GENESIS 1:26–27 ESV

Nothing will boost our confidence like realizing we're created in Your image, Father. It's not just our body, but our thoughts, too. We won't ever have to worry about our looks when our thoughts are firmly fastened on the things that please You. May this concept invigorate my own spiritual walk and that of my child, as well. Amen.

CHAPTER ELEVEN

Future

When we're young, we can't wait for tomorrow. We have so many plans, so many wishes, wants, and dreams. We know exactly what we want to do, when we want to do it, and where. What dreamers we are! If only tomorrow would come today, then we would be so happy.

As parents, however, we wish the clock would slow down. We beg God for more time. We cry as we pack our child's baby clothes in boxes and put them in the attic. We don't like the idea that our little ones will one day drive, date, or (gasp!) get married. The very idea makes us want to curl up in a ball. Why can't our little ones stay little? It seems so unfair. Yet, we know in our heart of hearts that God has big things for them. We don't want to get in the way of that, of course. There's a beautiful future ahead, and we get to witness it firsthand. What a privilege.

So, how do we pray for our child's future? First, we have to acknowledge that, while we can't see into tomorrow, God can. He knows what—and who—our children will be when they grow up. His plans probably don't match those that we've made for our kids, either. We might dream of having a doctor in the family; He might dream of having a missionary willing to move to Zambia. (Does that idea make you sweat, parents?) Truth is: God has amazing plans that far exceed any we might have for our children.

This chapter contains prayer prompts for the following topics: plans for the future, hope, a blameless walk, and many more. It's not enough to set our plans in motion. We have to be willing to take our hands off and let God have His way. As we commit to pray about our children's future, it gets easier and easier to do that, because we learn to trust that God has their best interest at heart. His calling is sure.

God's plans for our children are going to be wonderful, and we get to watch them unfold, right before our very eyes! That's why we take the time to pray about the road ahead, because it's going to be very exciting.

Of course, we also need to pray for our child's future spouse, but don't panic, parents! We'll cover that one in a later chapter. For now, let's hit our knees and ask the Lord to guide our kiddos as they head out into that vast unknown. . .the future.

Plans for the Future

"For I know the plans I have for you," declares the LORD,
"plans to prosper you and not to harm you,
plans to give you hope and a future."
JEREMIAH 29:11 NIV

I remember as a child wishing I could see into the future, Lord. Now that I'm grown, I'm so glad that wish never came true. Sometimes it's fun to think about what my child will be like when he's grown up. I don't know what his future will be like, but You do. You know where he will work, whom he will marry, and what sort of impact he will have on the kingdom of God. One thing is for sure. . . You have great plans for my child and I am forever grateful. Praise You, Lord! Amen.

Established Plans

Commit your work to the LORD,
and your plans will be established.
PROVERBS 16:3 ESV

You're the one who establishes our plans, Lord. You've given me a wonderful future and now my child faces a bright future, as well. I know he will go far because he's committing his work to You. You're helping him establish his plans so that he doesn't get off course. On those days when he doesn't feel like following through, please give him a little nudge. Remind him that You've called him to be a man of his word. His plans will be established as long as he sticks with You. Amen.

A Future Hope

Know also that wisdom is like honey for you:
If you find it, there is a future hope for you,
and your hope will not be cut off.
PROVERBS 24:14 NIV

I find it so interesting to think that godly wisdom plays a role in stirring up hope for the future, Father. Hope is a wonderful commodity. I know I couldn't live without it! Neither can my child. When I think about her future, I see that my counsel—good, godly counsel—will go a long way in bringing hope. When she's facing challenges, may my words bring hope, not pain. When she's struggling, may my counsel build her up, not tear her down. What a bright future she will have, Lord! Amen.

Observe the Upright

Consider the blameless, observe the upright;
a future awaits those who seek peace.
PSALM 37:37 NIV

Peace-seekers. We need more of those in this world, Lord. With so much chaos going on around the globe, peace-seekers are harder and harder to find. More often than not, people retaliate, returning an eye for an eye. I pray that my child will be a peace-seeker all of her days. Her future will be much brighter if she chooses to build bridges in relationships, to offer forgiveness when hurt, and live a blameless life, even when provoked. Help me to lead by example, Lord, so that my future will be bright, too. Amen.

The Purpose of the Lord

Many are the plans in the mind of a man,
but it is the purpose of the LORD that will stand.
PROVERBS 19:21 ESV

Sometimes I feel like my child is caught in a maze, Lord. So many plans, so little time! So much to do, so few hours to get it done. She works hard at so many things, some for play and others for academic purposes. Which of these things will stand the test of time and point her toward a future? That's for You to determine. I know that You see her future, Lord. You see beyond the "many plans" of today, to where she will be in ten, twenty, even fifty years. Thank You for the promise that Your purpose will stand. Amen.

These Stones

He said to the Israelites, "In the future when your descendants
ask their parents, 'What do these stones mean?' tell them,
'Israel crossed the Jordan on dry ground.'"
JOSHUA 4:21–22 NIV

Oh, the stories we parents have to tell! When my children are grown, Lord, I plan to share them all—the silly ones, the "remember when" ones. . .all of them! I love this verse because it reminds me that I also need to tell my children stories about the marvelous things You've done in our family's past. Why? So that they can see that You are for us, not against us. You've been there for us in the past and will give us a remarkable future if we do not wander from You. Thank You for that promise, Lord. Amen.

The Way You Should Go

I will instruct you and teach you in the way you should go;
I will counsel you with my eye upon you.
PSALM 32:8 NIV

As I think about my child's future, I'm reminded that she has to be given parameters, Lord. If I give her too wide a berth, she could go off course. I don't want to be overly strict, but I do need to keep an eye on things to make sure her course is sure. I need to offer godly counsel. This comes straight from Your heart, Father! It all starts with You. Please guide my steps so that I can help guide hers. Amen.

Mark the Blameless

Mark the blameless and behold the upright,
for there is a future for the man of peace.
PSALM 37:37 ESV

I remember what it was like to be a kid, Lord. We always seemed to be pointing fingers at one another, shifting the blame. Never accepting responsibility. Today's scripture has reminded me that I need to teach my child to be blameless. I need to encourage him to "own it" when he's messed up, to be blameless in all he does. When he steps up and does the right thing, it assures a wonderful future for him. Help me as I share this concept with him, Lord. Amen.

Your Will Be Done

"Your kingdom come, your will be done,
on earth as it is in heaven."
MATTHEW 6:10 ESV

It's all about Your will, Father. Help me to see this in my everyday life, and help me to pass that concept along to my children, as well. When we seek first Your kingdom, when we ask for Your will to be done, then our future will be bright. When we seek first our own will, follow after things that gratify the flesh or (supposedly) fill the empty void in our hearts, our future looks bleak. I want a bright future for my children, Father, so I'm committed to seeking Your kingdom, Your will. Amen.

⎯⎯∞⎯⎯

His Workmanship

For we are his workmanship, created in Christ Jesus for good works,
which God prepared beforehand, that we should walk in them.
EPHESIANS 2:10 ESV

You went to a lot of trouble to create each of us, Lord. We're individual for a reason. As different as we all might be on the outside, there's one thing that unifies us on the inside: we were all created to do great things, not for ourselves, but for You. My child is Your workmanship. (Great job, Lord!) He's specially crafted. Now stir up that "good works" mentality so that he can step out in faith and do mighty things in Your name. Amen!

Never Forsaken

I have been young, and now am old, yet I have not seen
the righteous forsaken or his children begging for bread.
PSALM 37:25 ESV

Sometimes we worry about the future, Lord. Finances are tight. Things don't always turn out like we plan. I wonder if my kids will have the things they need. In other words, I doubt Your Word. I forget to trust. Then I read a scripture like this one and I'm reminded that You never forsake us. Sure, finances might be tight at times. Sure, my kids might not have the latest, greatest electronic gizmos. Still, they have something far greater, Lord. . .the assurance that You will always take care of us and meet our every need. What a loving Father You are! Amen.

Brought to Completion

And I am sure of this, that he who began a good work in
you will bring it to completion at the day of Jesus Christ.
PHILIPPIANS 1:6 ESV

You don't give up on us, Lord. No matter how badly we fail, how far we fall, You don't give up. You bring us to completion. Sometimes I look at my children—especially the ones who struggle most—and wonder what sort of future they will have. I worry. I think, "This one's got a tough road ahead of him," or "That one's challenges are too great." Then I'm reminded of this truth: if You start something, Lord. . .You will finish it. I have nothing to worry about. You've got this, and I'm so grateful. Amen!

Just a Word

It was by faith that Isaac promised blessings
for the future to his sons, Jacob and Esau.
HEBREWS 11:20 NLT

It takes faith to trust that we have a bright future. I see this, even in the men and women I read about in the Bible. Isaac had faith when he blessed his two sons. He felt sure their futures would be great. I need to be just as confident as I pass off blessings to my children. Help me to speak confidently and boldly about all of the great things You have in store for them, Lord. I can give them hope for great days ahead with just a word. Thanks for this reminder. Amen.

———

Wings Like Eagles

But those who hope in the LORD will renew their strength.
They will soar on wings like eagles; they will run and
not grow weary, they will walk and not be faint.
ISAIAH 40:31 NIV

My child has so much to look forward to, Lord. I see her years from now, making a difference in this world. In order to accomplish that, she needs Your renewed strength. That's what I pray for her today, Father. As she places her hope in You, please reignite, reinvigorate, renew her heart and her strength. All things new, Lord! Then she can soar toward the goal, energized to do great things for You. Amen.

CHAPTER TWELVE

Forgiveness

A very forgiving woman once shared a story about her childhood. She was raised in a home with abusive parents. They treated her deplorably. She was badly beaten and even lit on fire at one point, then left to die. As parents, we are horrified by such stories. Sadly, they do exist.

You would think that a woman like this would grow bitter, angry, and resentful. She would have every right to hate her perpetrators and to wish for bad things to happen to them. Instead, this woman chose to forgive. She said that forgiveness was like taking a key and opening a locked cage. The person inside—the one who committed the offense—would be set free, yes, but so would the one doing the forgiving.

When we choose to forgive, we are really releasing ourselves—from the bitterness, the unforgiveness, and the hard heart. It's difficult to imagine forgiving such atrocities, but sometimes we have trouble forgiving the little things, too. For instance, we can't seem to forgive ourselves for harsh words spoken over our kids. We can't seem to forgive a spouse who disagrees with us about how our children should be raised. We can't forgive the kid down the block who excluded our child. On and on it goes. We hang on to our unforgiveness, convinced we are right. We want to be strong for the sake of our child. Who else will take a stand for him, if not us?

Oh, parents, how we need to learn to forgive. How we need to teach this principle to our children. Pastor T. D. Jakes put it this way: "We think that forgiveness is weakness, but it's absolutely not; it takes a very strong person to forgive."

Think about that for a moment. We all want to be strong. We can see that holding someone in unforgiveness holds us back, as well. So, we must reach the inevitable point where we're willing to let go—to forgive. To let God deal with the person in his own time and his own way.

How do we teach our children to forgive? Like us, they experience wounds. People hurt their feelings. They put up walls. What they do with those walls depends, in part, on us. Our children are watching how we deal with the walls in our own lives. They are looking to see how we handle bitterness and pain. They're emulating our behavior.

Oh boy. Looks like we have a lot of work to do. Better get busy praying, not just for our kiddos but ourselves, as well.

Forgiving One Another

Be kind and compassionate to one another,
forgiving each other, just as in Christ God forgave you.
EPHESIANS 4:32 NIV

Forgiveness doesn't always come easy, Lord. I know You know this better than anyone. You had to forgive those who hated Your Son. It's hard for me to forgive people who've hurt my child, too. When they say or do mean things, the bear in me wants to come out. Help me to guard myself, Father, and to forgive. Help me to teach my child to do the same, even when it's really, really difficult. Thank You for leading by example, Lord. Amen.

Forgive. . .and Be Forgiven

"For if you forgive other people when they sin against you,
your heavenly Father will also forgive you. But if you do not
forgive men their sins, your Father will not forgive your sins."
MATTHEW 6:14–15 NIV

Sometimes we hang on to pain far too long, Lord. I see my child struggling with this at times. She lets things linger. She gets worked up and won't let go of the ugly things that people have said or done to her. They become a part of her. It's not that she's trying to retaliate or return evil for evil. She truly just can't seem to let go. Show me how to minister to her, Father, so that she can walk through the process of both forgiving and letting go. Ultimately, it will be a win-win situation. Amen.

Over and Over Again

Then Peter came to Jesus and asked, "Lord, how many times shall I forgive my brother or sister who sins against me? Up to seven times?" Jesus answered, "I tell you, not seven times, but seventy-seven times."
MATTHEW 18:21–22 NIV

When you're friends with someone for a long period of time, you're bound to clash at times. Disagreements come, even with the best of friends. I know this, Lord! I've lived through it. My child has experienced this with his friends, too. They're fine one minute, then bickering and arguing the next. Show me how to lead by example when it comes to the forgiveness issue. The "seventy times seven" rule applies to parents, too, not just kids! Amen.

What Goes Around

"Do not judge, and you will not be judged. Do not condemn, and you will not be condemned. Forgive, and you will be forgiven."
LUKE 6:37 NIV

We live in such a judgmental world, Lord. People are always judging others by appearance, financial standing, even cultures. It's so hard to get around it. Thank You for reminding me that we're not called to be judge and jury. If we don't want others to judge us, we can't judge them. If we don't want them to cut us down, we can't cut them down. If we want to be forgiven, we must forgive. Help me, Father, as I convey this message to my child. Amen.

How to Treat Enemies

On the contrary: "If your enemy is hungry, feed him;
if he is thirsty, give him something to drink.
In doing this, you will heap burning coals on his head."
ROMANS 12:20 NIV

Oh, it's hard to be kind to some people, Lord! They make it so difficult!
Yet Your Word makes it clear: we're called to reach out to all people,
not just the ones who are easy. It's the difficult ones we're called to
feed when hungry. It's the tough cases to whom we're expected to offer
water when thirsty. When we treat the difficult people with love and
kindness, it changes everything. I'm determined to keep trying, Father,
so that my kids can learn from my example. It's not easy, but I'm working on it! Help me, I pray. Amen.

A Healthy Confession

Therefore, confess your sins to one another and pray for
one another, that you may be healed. The prayer of a
righteous person has great power as it is working.
JAMES 5:16 ESV

We've heard it all our lives, Lord: confession is good for the soul. This
is true at every age, but it's often difficult. I've seen my child hide her
sins and flaws, afraid of repercussions. Please help me as I guide her
down a path toward confession and forgiveness. Show her that getting
things out in the open is always for the best, even when she's dealing
with shame. If she can confess it, she can learn to forgive herself. If
she learns to forgive herself, she will eventually learn to forgive others
when they hurt her. Thank You for extending Your grace, Lord. Amen.

Washed Clean

And Peter said to them, "Repent and be baptized every one of
you in the name of Jesus Christ for the forgiveness of your sins,
and you will receive the gift of the Holy Spirit."
ACTS 2:38 ESV

When we come into relationship with You, Lord, You wash us clean.
We give You our hearts—dirty, stained—and You replace them with
clean, pure ones. Your forgiveness extends far beyond any sin we've
committed. Everything is washed away. Our external baptism symbol-
izes what's taken place inside: the old has become new! Today I pray
that my child will walk in complete forgiveness and that his heart will
remain fixed to Yours. Thank You for Your work on the cross, Lord.
Amen.

Lead Us Not into Temptation

"And forgive us our sins, for we ourselves also forgive
everyone who is indebted to us. And lead us not into temptation."
LUKE 11:4 NASB

Sometimes we get into a vicious cycle, Lord. We forgive ourselves for
something we've done wrong, and then we get pulled into temptation
and do that "bad thing" again. My child struggles with this. Tempta-
tions abound, and she's walked right into a few, eyes wide open. I've
seen her fall and then get back up, only to fall again. Please encourage
her heart today, Lord. Show her that You keep on forgiving. Then lead
her away from temptation, Father, so that the cycle can be broken.
Amen.

The Greatest Example

*But Jesus was saying, "Father, forgive them; for they do
not know what they are doing." And they cast lots,
dividing up His garments among themselves.*
LUKE 23:34 NASB

There will never be a greater example of forgiveness than You, Jesus!
When You died on the cross, You performed the greatest sacrifice in
all of history. Your blood spilled out to forgive my sins, my child's sins,
and the sins of many generations both past and present. How can we
thank You, Lord? We can only vow to live lives of forgiveness, as well.
Praise You for your work on Calvary! Amen.

While We Were Yet Sinners

*But God demonstrates His own love toward us,
in that while we were yet sinners, Christ died for us.*
ROMANS 5:8 NASB

It's one thing to be kind and forgiving to someone who's genuinely
good. It's a lot harder to bestow forgiveness on someone who keeps
messing up, over and over again. Yet You showed us how to do that,
Lord, when You forgave us! Now help me spread that message to my
children. May they come to understand that even the "toughest case"
is worthy of Your forgiveness. . .and theirs, too. Thank You for that
reminder today, Lord. Amen.

Caught!

Brethren, even if anyone is caught in any trespass, you who are
spiritual, restore such a one in a spirit of gentleness;
each one looking to yourself, so that you too will not be tempted.
GALATIANS 6:1 NASB

It seems I'm always catching my child in "trespasses," Lord. I'm always correcting him, one lecture after another. I'm sure this wears him down. It certainly wears me down! Today I ask that You would help me restore him in a spirit of gentleness, as this scripture says. Calm my spirit and my verbal and physical responses. Guard my heart, Lord. . . and his, too. Amen.

Preserving Unity

Therefore I, the prisoner of the Lord, implore you to walk in a manner
worthy of the calling with which you have been called, with all humility
and gentleness, with patience, showing tolerance for one another in love,
being diligent to preserve the unity of the Spirit in the bond of peace.
EPHESIANS 4:1–3 NASB

Believers are called to walk in unity, Lord, and it's not always easy. We have disagreements about pretty much everything. If we're not careful, things blow up. Feelings get hurt. Words are spoken. Friends are wounded. Our children are watching. Help me, Father, as I navigate this path with my Christian brothers and sisters. May we always walk in forgiveness and grace so that our children learn by example. Amen.

Selfishness, Be Gone!

Do nothing from selfishness or empty conceit but with humility of mind regard one another as more important than yourselves; do not merely look out for your own personal interests, but also for the interests of others.
PHILIPPIANS 2:3–4 NASB

It's easy to forgive when we put others first, Lord. It's hard when we're "I, me, my" focused. Sometimes I get so busy looking after my own interests and the interests of my child that I can't see what's best for those around us. I'm only thinking of us. Help me to have a broader vision, Lord. You love us all, and want what's best for everyone. Help me to lay down my selfishness today so that my child—and our friends—can benefit. Amen.

———

Persevere

Blessed is a man who perseveres under trial; for once he has been approved, he will receive the crown of life which the Lord has promised to those who love Him.
JAMES 1:12 NASB

Forgiveness and perseverance often go hand in hand, Lord. To walk with someone through thick and thin means forgiving and then trying again. I love this promise in Your Word that says a crown is coming for those who persevere. My child is learning how to do this, too. She's had her ups and downs in relationships, but perseveres. Help her, Lord. May she keep on keeping on, even when things get tough. Amen.

CHAPTER THIRTEEN

Loving Others

Loving comes naturally when you're a parent. You look down at that newborn babe in your arms and your heart is filled with an instantaneous affection for her. She's so easy to love because she's part of you. She's God's gift to you.

Yes, our children are (mostly) easy to love. What about their friends? Their teachers? What about the parent down the block. . .the one who espouses a passionate (opposite) view of parenting? What about the Little League coach who picks on our kid? Are these people just as easy to love? Not always.

It's time to admit the truth, parents. We love our kids, but we don't always love the people around them. We want the best for our kiddo, but we don't always want the best for the child sitting next to him on the playground.

It's time for a heart change. Love doesn't have a "my kid first" or "my family first" attitude. When we begin to see others as God sees them—when we begin to love them as He loves them—it will change not only our perspective, but our child's, as well.

Love isn't an emotion. It's a choice. In much the same way that we choose to pray when we don't feel like it, we also choose to love when we don't feel like it. We teach our children to do the same—even when they're hurt by kids on the playground who call them names. Even when they're ignored or overlooked by a teacher or coach.

We learn how to love the unlovable by watching how God

loves us when our behavior is less than stellar. He doesn't give up on us. He calls out to us, wooing us back to Himself. He only asks two things of us in response: to love Him with all our heart, soul, mind, and strength, and to love others as we love ourselves.

So, how do we pray for our children to love this way? Love definitely isn't something you can fake your way through. If it's not genuine, it won't change lives. Start by recommitting yourself to loving God with your whole heart. Enter into His throne room with words of love on your lips. Then your love for others (even that naughty kid down the street) will come easier. Speak words of love over your children. Teach them to adore their heavenly Father and then watch as that love spills over onto their peers.

Ready to get serious about loving others? Let's pray.

Because He First Loved Us

We love because he first loved us.
1 JOHN 4:19 NIV

Your love propels us, Lord! It gives us the courage—the audacity—to love the unlovable, to forgive the unpardonable, to speak to mountains, to see our futures as hopeful. There's nothing like the love of God to change a life, to mend marriages, to help broken families. I'm so thankful for Your love today, Lord. May my children experience it in all of its fullness, so that their hearts can leap for joy as mine does now. Amen.

Love's Perfect Order

Jesus replied: " 'Love the Lord your God with all your heart and with all your soul and with all your mind.' This is the first and greatest commandment. And the second is like it: 'Love your neighbor as yourself.' "
MATTHEW 22:37–39 NIV

I'm learning that love has an order, Father. We love You first. This comes easily. Then we love our neighbor. This isn't always so easy! I love the part of the verse that says "as yourself" because there's an implication that we're called to love ourselves, too. Please help me show my child how to exhibit an "others first" sort of love, but help me keep this teaching in balance, Lord, so that he knows to love himself as well. I'm so grateful for Your love, Father! Amen.

The Proof's in the Loving

But love your enemies, do good to them, and lend to them without expect-
ing to get anything back. Then your reward will be great, and you will be
children of the Most High, because he is kind to the ungrateful and wicked.
LUKE 6:35 NIV

How do we show love to our enemies, Lord? This is a question my
child has asked. She wants to get back at the ones who hurt her, but
loving them is Your answer. I see the answer to her dilemma in this
verse! She must do good to them without expecting to get anything
back. Wow. I'm going to need Your help as I teach her this concept,
Father. It's a tough one! Please help me, as I show her that the reward
will be great as she loves her enemies. Amen.

Never-failing Love

Love is patient, love is kind. It does not envy, it does not boast,
it is not proud. It does not dishonor others, it is not self-seeking,
it is not easily angered, it keeps no record of wrongs. Love does
not delight in evil but rejoices with the truth. It always protects,
always trusts, always hopes, always perseveres. Love never fails.
But where there are prophecies, they will cease; where there are tongues,
they will be stilled; where there is knowledge, it will pass away.
1 CORINTHIANS 13:4–8 NIV

What a powerful verse, Lord. Today I repeat the words to this verse
aloud, speaking them over my child's life. May she be patient and kind.
May she turn away from envy and give up on boasting. May she lay
down her pride and give up rudeness. May she seek You first, others
second, and may her temper always be in check. May she trust, hope,
and persevere. Oh, Lord. . .thank You for this amazing definition of
love! Amen.

The Greatest Is Love

And now these three remain: faith, hope and love.
But the greatest of these is love.
1 CORINTHIANS 13:13 NIV

I'm working hard to teach my child about faith, Lord. It's easier to talk about than to live out sometimes! I'm teaching him about hope, too. . .about a bright future. But love, Lord? This is the thing I most want to instill in my child. Not an earthly love—"I love this cheeseburger" or "I love my new computer." The kind of love I want to instill in him is the "forever" version. Your love. Helping him understand Your love is truly the greatest gift I can give him.

Love Covers Sins

Above all, love each other deeply,
because love covers over a multitude of sins.
1 PETER 4:8 NIV

Love covers sins. What a wonderful thought, Lord! Love has the power to wipe away even the worst blemishes. When I love my child as You love me, I will extend grace. Forgiveness. I won't overreact or snap at her. I won't get hung up on things that are non-eternal. When I love as You love, I will help her through the mess-ups and give her encouragement to try again. I need Your help with all of this, Father. Because I know You love me, I feel confident You will give it. Praise You for that! Amen.

Love Cares More About Others

Greater love has no one than this:
to lay down one's life for one's friends.
JOHN 15:13 NIV

I've wrestled with this verse for years, Father. What does it mean to lay down your life for someone? It goes against our nature to lay down our lives, but that's the very thing You've called us to do. How do I do that, and how do I teach my child by example? I know it begins with laying down selfishness, but what else? Show me, in my relationships, when to give of myself to others. Teach me how to have an "others first" attitude. Help my child live a sacrificial life, too. Give us wisdom, O Lord, that we might be a blessing to others. Amen.

Love the Brotherhood

Honour all men. Love the brotherhood.
Fear God. Honour the king.
1 PETER 2:17 KJV

You've given us brothers and sisters in the Lord to love, to encourage, and to befriend. I pray that my child will see his godly friends as the gift they are. May he never see our church family as anything but a true "brotherhood" (a place where you can let your hair down, be yourself). May his love for his Christian friends remain for years to come. Thank You, Lord, for godly relationships, both for my child and for me. We're so grateful. Amen.

There's Strength in Love

I love you, LORD, my strength.
PSALM 18:1 NIV

What a wonderful verse, Lord! Just a few simple words, but they say so much: "I love you, O Lord, my strength." *You* are my strength, Lord. You and You alone. This is what I need to teach my child. You are her strength, too. She wants to become a stronger student, a stronger athlete, and to have stronger friendships. The source of strength comes from loving You. What a simple but profound concept. May she grow stronger and stronger each day as her love for You deepens. Amen.

Undivided

Hatred stirs up conflict,
but love covers over all wrongs.
PROVERBS 10:12 NIV

Love tears down barriers, Lord. I've seen this in my relationships. I've seen this in my family. I've seen this in my church. Hatred stirs up dissension, but love covers wrongs. It embraces instead of pushing away. It does away with differences and points out the things we have in common. I pray that my child would come to know this kind of barrier-breaking love today, Father! Let me lead by example, I pray. Amen.

Heart, Soul, Might

And thou shalt love the LORD thy God with all thine heart,
and with all thy soul, and with all thy might.
DEUTERONOMY 6:5 KJV

What an interesting picture, Lord! We're not just called to love You, but to love You forcefully—with heart. With soul. With might! We love You with determination, by choice. We're not coerced into loving. We do it because we feel Your love for us. This is my prayer for my child, Father! I don't ever want him to feel like I'm forcing him to believe in You or to love You. May he sense Your love so strongly that He runs to You, loving with heart, soul, and strength! Amen.

A New Commandment

"A new commandment I give to you, that you love one another:
just as I have loved you, you also are to love one another."
JOHN 13:34 ESV

Love isn't a new concept, Lord. You've loved mankind since the beginning of time. Yet with each new day we're faced with loving people all over again. In a sense, it's a new commandment each morning when our feet hit the ground. May my child forget the problems (and disagreements) of yesterday. May she awaken today with love for others. May the "newness" of Your love grab hold of her today as she comes in contact with both the loveable. . .and the unlovable. Amen.

Fruity

But the fruit of the Spirit is love, joy, peace,
longsuffering, gentleness, goodness, faith.
GALATIANS 5:22 KJV

I get it, Lord! Love is one of the fruits of the Spirit. It's a natural by-product of being in relationship with You. If I stick close to You, then loving others will be easier. Now help me teach this to my child, Father! When it's not easy to love those she comes in contact with, remind her that she's called to be "fruity" (to be a witness of Your love). Propel her to love others, I pray, and make her fruitful in all of her relationships. Thank You, Lord. Amen.

⸺

Royalty

If you really fulfill the royal law according to the Scripture,
"You shall love your neighbor as yourself," you are doing well.
JAMES 2:8 ESV

Love is the royal law. I've never really grasped that idea before, Lord, but I'm seeing it now through Your eyes. It's a heavenly concept, to love others as we love ourselves. It's not something that comes from our earthy, human nature. It takes divine intervention to love this way! Today I pray that You would teach my child this concept. May she learn to love the way You love—with others taking precedence. Give her a divine revelation of how she can live this way, not just today, but for the rest of her life. Amen.

CHAPTER FOURTEEN

Generosity/Kindness

—

Parents, we need to recommit ourselves to kindness, to generosity. We need to teach our children to be kind. The great John Bunyan (author of *Pilgrim's Progress*) said it best: "You have not lived today until you have done something for someone who can never repay you." That quote flies in the face of modern philosophies, doesn't it? Oh, but it shouldn't! Kindness and generosity should be a natural part of who we are as believers.

Kindness starts with consideration. This is where many of us go wrong. To be considerate means our eyes are on the other guy, not ourselves. We're "considering" him before we "consider" ourselves. Oh, how difficult this is, especially when we're parents! We want what's best for our child. Our child's team. Our child's classroom. Our child's circle of friends. Sure, we're kind to those in the inner circle, but does our kindness spill over to the rival team? To those we disagree with? To the neighbor who drives us crazy mowing his lawn at the crack of dawn? We don't want to "consider" these people. They don't make the "kindness list." We nudge them off and focus on the ones who really matter to us.

It should not be, parents! Jesus taught us by example to be kindhearted. To be kindhearted means we're friendly. We're considerate. We don't just see our own interests, but care about the interests of others. When we're kind, we go out of our way to be warmhearted, to show affection. We're thoughtful and unselfish, sympathetic and understanding. We're big-hearted. Neighborly. (Kindness sounds a lot like love, doesn't it?)

Kindness and generosity go hand in hand. Think about what it means to be neighborly. A "neighborly" person shows up at your door with a casserole in her hand when you're sick. She gives, not out of obligation, but because she's close by and sees what's going on. There are many people who are "close by" your family. Can you see their needs? Are you training your children to reach out a hand of friendship and kindness?

Before we pray for our children to be kind, we might need to start by examining our own hearts. Praying, "Lord, make me a better neighbor" might be a great start, followed by, "Give me a kind, generous heart." He will do it! He will show you how to pray for your child, so that generosity spills over on his peers.

Are you ready, parents? This one might require a bit of sacrifice, but the payoff will be great. Ready, set. . .pray!

Kindness for Kindness

"Do to others as you would have them do to you."
LUKE 6:31 NIV

We've heard it all our lives, Father: "What goes around comes around."
My child is just learning this principle. When he's kind to others, they
are kind to him. Not always, of course, but usually. Remind him when
he's around not-so-kind kids (at school, at church, on the playground)
that he can start the cycle of kindness by being the first one to respond
generously. He has the power to turn that situation around with just a
word. Speak to his heart and give him the courage to be kind. Amen.

Put It On

So, as those who have been chosen of God, holy and beloved,
put on a heart of compassion, kindness,
humility, gentleness and patience.
COLOSSIANS 3:12 NASB

Lord, while my child is dressing for the day, remind her to "put on"
compassion for those in need. Kindness, for those who need a kind
word. Humility, so that she doesn't come across as a show-off. Gentleness, both with her peers and her teachers and mentors. Patience,
with all she comes in contact. What she wears on the inside is far more
important than the clothes she wears on the outside. May she never
forget this. Amen.

A Necklace of Kindness

Do not let kindness and truth leave you;
Bind them around your neck,
write them on the tablet of your heart.
PROVERBS 3:3 NASB

I love this verse, Lord. It helps me picture kindness as a necklace, something close to the heart and close to the lips! When our hearts are right with You, kind words will flow from our mouths. As my children spend time with their peers, help them to see that they can carry kindness and truth with them—to school, to church. . .everywhere. The "necklace" of kindness and truth will guard their hearts. What a lovely image, Father! Thank You for this beautiful necklace. Amen.

A Giving Heart

Each of you should give what you have decided in your heart to give,
not reluctantly or under compulsion, for God loves a cheerful giver.
2 CORINTHIANS 9:7 NIV

Generosity and kindness go hand in hand, don't they, Lord? When we want to show kindness, we can't help but give. When we see others in need, we're compelled to give even more. I'm so grateful that I can teach my child to be generous. What a lovely way to show kindness. Place someone in our path who could benefit from my child's generosity, I pray. May he live this lesson out loud, Father. Amen.

Hospitality to Strangers

Do not neglect to show hospitality to strangers,
for by this some have entertained angels without knowing it.
HEBREWS 13:2 NASB

I'm enjoying the process of teaching my child hospitality, Father. She's enjoying it, too. She loves caring for others, especially those who really need her. I'm blessed as I watch her give so selflessly. I'm reminded as I read this verse that my daughter's hospitality has far-reaching effects. As she reaches out to others, she could be entertaining angels unaware. What an amazing thought, Lord. Thank You for instilling generosity in her heart. Amen.

Put It into Action!

And I am praying that you will put into action the
generosity that comes from your faith as you understand
and experience all the good things we have in Christ.
PHILEMON 1:6 NLT

It's one thing to want to be generous; it's another to actually follow through. When I totally place my trust in You, Lord, I'm more apt to give. When I'm walking in fear, I hold back. I don't want my child to be motivated by fear. I want to show her that we can trust You to provide for our every need. We don't give to receive, but when we do give, we trust. Help me to put generosity into action in my life so that my children will see. . .and respond. Amen.

What I Do Have

As a result of your ministry, they will give glory to God.
For your generosity to them and to all believers will
prove that you are obedient to the Good News of Christ.
2 CORINTHIANS 9:13 NLT

I want to teach my child to be obedient to You, Lord. You've asked us to give generously, and I want to lead by example. I don't always have a lot of money to give, but I have other things: time, talents, and treasures. I can share these things in my local church and show my child that we have more to offer than just our pocketbooks. Stir up the gifts in my child so that he can give his time, talents, and treasures, too. May his generosity make a difference, both now and in the future. Amen.

Cheerfully

If it is to encourage, then give encouragement; if it is giving,
then give generously; if it is to lead, do it diligently;
if it is to show mercy, do it cheerfully.
ROMANS 12:8 NIV

I love the joy on my child's face when she gives, Lord. She enjoys the process of helping others. When I think of her sweet, giving nature, I'm especially grateful. She's responding to the call to help others, and that makes me very, very proud. She's doing it all cheerfully! She's leading others (even me) by example. What a precious woman of God she is. Thank You so much for her generosity. Amen.

Making Things Right

"Don't be afraid," David said to him, "for I will surely show you kindness
for the sake of your father Jonathan. I will restore to you all the land that
belonged to your grandfather Saul, and you will always eat at my table."
2 SAMUEL 9:7 NIV

I love this verse about David showing kindness for the sake of his old friend, Jonathan. What a beautiful story of grace, Father! May I learn to extend this kind of generosity to those around me who've been cheated in one way or another—to the friend without a spouse. To the elderly widowed neighbor. To the child without a father. While I'm caring for those in need, may my children learn to do the same. Thank You for opening our eyes to the great needs in our community so that we can share Your love. Amen.

Kindness Leads to Repentance

Or do you think lightly of the riches of His kindness and tolerance
and patience, not knowing that the kindness
of God leads you to repentance?
ROMANS 2:4 NASB

We learn to be kind by following Your lead, Lord. We don't take what You did on the cross lightly. Sending Your Son to die in our place was the greatest act of kindness ever shown to mankind. In turn, I must be kind. I must teach my kids to be kind. It's Your kindness that leads us to repentance. When we see how beautifully You've treated us in the past, we have hope for the future. Touch my child's heart today, Father, and remind him where true kindness comes from. Amen.

What the Lord Requires

He has told you, O man, what is good;
And what does the LORD require of you but to do justice,
to love kindness, and to walk humbly with your God?
MICAH 6:8 NASB

You've told us what is good, Lord. Justice is good. Kindness is good. Humility in our walk with You is good. I pray that my child grows to understand justice (Your version of it). I pray that he learns to appreciate humility. I pray that his ability to show kindness grows exponentially over the years. These "requirements" assure us a happy, productive life—a life of which we can be proud. I'm already proud, just thinking of the possibilities for my child. Amen.

He Won't Forget

For God is not unjust so as to forget your work
and the love which you have shown toward His name,
in having ministered and in still ministering to the saints.
HEBREWS 6:10 NASB

Showing kindness is a good thing. Generosity is a good thing. Both of those things can be taxing at times. That's why I love this scripture, Father. You see my workload. You know what I'm facing. You won't forget my work. You won't forget my love for others. I pray that my child knows You're watching, too. May she never feel taken advantage of as she ministers to others. May she always know that You're looking down on her kindness and smiling. What a wonderful Father You are! Amen.

The House of Faith

So then, as we have opportunity, let us do good to everyone,
and especially to those who are of the household of faith.
GALATIANS 6:10 ESV

We love our church, Lord! It's a great place to worship corporately and to learn about Your precepts with fellow believers. Thank You for this reminder that it's especially important to do good for those in the "household of faith" (our fellow believers, both inside church walls and out). We're family! My child is a part of that wonderful family, so strengthen his desire to help when help is needed, to encourage when encouragement is called for, and to do good at all times to his Christian brothers and sisters. Amen.

Burden Bearers

Bear one another's burdens,
and so fulfill the law of Christ.
GALATIANS 6:2 ESV

It's rarely fun to bear the burdens of someone in pain, Father. I've done it several times and it can be weighty. Yet the benefits far outweigh the pain, if not in the short-term, then in the long. Though it's not easy, I do want to pass on the willingness to do this to my child, not so that she can become a doormat, but so she can really be there when a friend in need comes calling. May she choose carefully who to allow this special privilege, Father. Protect her generous, kind heart, I pray. Give her wisdom to speak into the lives of those to whom she ministers. Amen.

CHAPTER FIFTEEN

Godly Wisdom

Let's face it, parents: we want our kids to be smart. We want them to do well in school, to excel academically, and to go on to college so that they can have great careers. We spend a lot of time training them to be excellent students, even pitting them against other kids along the way, so that they can get the better scholarships, better schools, better everything. "Smarts" are in. Wisdom? Well, sometimes we overlook that one. Why? Because we're convinced knowledge and wisdom are one and the same. Nothing could be further from the truth.

There's a huge difference between knowledge and wisdom. Knowledge (worldly wisdom) can take our children far in this world. It can root them in the perfect school, the ideal job. Yet if our child doesn't have godly wisdom, none of that will matter. They might land the perfect job, and then fall flat because they don't have godly wisdom to make good decisions in the moment.

How do we pray for our child to become wise? We need to start by recognizing the difference between the world's version of wisdom and God's. Knowledge (worldly wisdom) is based on human understanding. Wisdom flows down from the heart of God. Once we "get" the difference, we'll focus on the real goal: teaching our child how to pray for God's version of it.

There are biblical promises regarding wisdom. To "get" it, we have to teach our child to seek it. We also have to instill a love of the Bible. Meditating on God's Word is a key way to obtain godly wisdom. Listening to (and following) godly counsel is another way to "get" wisdom. (Let's be honest: Sometimes we struggle with this in our own lives.) As with all things, we teach by example. If we walk in wisdom, we will train our children to do so, as well.

The wisest decision our child can ever make is to give his heart to the Lord. Once he's walking in sync with the Author of wisdom, he will glean, glean, glean. Keeping him in the church, surrounded by godly people, helps, too. There he will learn from others who have godly mind-sets.

What about knowledge? Should we overlook academic "smarts" as wisdom takes precedence? Absolutely not. A kiddo who's both knowledgeable and wise will have great impact on his world.

Prepare yourselves, parents. This one's going to be a lot of work, but the payoff will be great. Ready to pray? Let's get going.

Walking with the Wise

He who walks with the wise will be wise,
but the companion of fools will suffer harm.
PROVERBS 13:20 NASB

Ah, wise friends! How we need them, Lord! Wise friends help pull us back from the edge of the cliff when we're about to go over. They speak truth—sometimes hard truth—into our lives when we're about to stray. They offer godly advice, words we can take to the bank. Today I pray that my child would attract wise friends and be a wise friend in return. May she draw people who think like You, and may she listen to sound advice. May they, together, seek to hear Your voice, so that wise choices can be made. Thank You for offering such godly wisdom, Lord. Amen.

A Message of Wisdom

We do, however, speak a message of wisdom among the mature,
but not the wisdom of this age or of the rulers of this age,
who are coming to nothing.
1 CORINTHIANS 2:6 NIV

Some people are clueless, Lord. You can talk to them about the Gospel all day long, but they simply don't get it. Many are too "smart" for their own good. They can't understand a message rooted in faith. I know that my child will come in contact with people like this in her life. I pray You would gird her up, even now, to be prepared. May she speak a message of wisdom straight from the heart, not at all concerned about how she's being judged by those who don't get it. I know that many will get it, Lord, and their lives will be changed. Thank You for that! Amen.

Wisdom to Please

Children, obey your parents in everything,
for this pleases the Lord.
COLOSSIANS 3:20 NIV

We all suffer from a lack of wisdom at times, Father. I know I do. My child does, too. Sometimes he goes off on a tangent and gets away from what he knows is best for him. He doesn't want to obey. I see rebellion rising up in his heart and it makes me sad. It also makes me very, very aware that the enemy is working overtime to bring division. Today I ask that You would give my child the wisdom he needs to obey. May he come to see that obedience pleases You, Father. Thank You for speaking to him, even when he's off doing his own thing. Amen.

Self-Controlled and Alert

Be alert and of sober mind. Your enemy the devil prowls
around like a roaring lion looking for someone to devour.
1 PETER 5:8 NIV

A wise person stays alert. I know this from reading Your Word, Father, and from my own experience. If we're not alert, the enemy comes in and attempts to wreak havoc. This is even true in our family life. If I'm not diligent to pray for my kids, if I'm not completely alert, the devil prowls around and seeks to devour. That's a scary image. . .until I remember that You are far greater than he is. Then I'm reminded that I have Your power living inside of me. Whew! That's good news, Father. Thank You for the wisdom to be alert. Amen.

Words of the Wise

Yet when I am among mature believers, I do speak with words
of wisdom, but not the kind of wisdom that belongs to this
world or to the rulers of this world, who are soon forgotten.
1 CORINTHIANS 2:6 NLT

It's so wonderful to hang out with other believers because we can talk
about the things of God and really connect over common interests. I'm
grateful that You've given my child believers to connect with, young
and old. Sunday school teachers. Mentors. Older children who care.
Peers. You've surrounded my child with wise people who will pour into
his life and offer sage advice, when needed. Their brand of wisdom goes
beyond anything the world has to offer. I'm so grateful for that. Thank
You, Lord. Amen.

Get It!

The beginning of wisdom is this: Get wisdom.
Though it cost all you have, get understanding.
PROVERBS 4:7 NIV

When I read today's verse I'm reminded of a television commercial,
Lord, one that encourages me to "get" a particular product. To "get"
something means I go after it with intention. I go to the store to buy a
certain item. I don't leave the store until I have it. That's how it is with
wisdom. I want my child to "get" it, to go after it and not give up until
she has it. There will be a cost involved, for sure. She'll have to focus
and give it her all. You will help her every step of the way. Praise You
for that, Father! Amen.

No Deficits

*If any of you is deficient in wisdom, let him ask of the giving God
[Who gives] to everyone liberally and ungrudgingly,
without reproaching or faultfinding, and it will be given him.*
JAMES 1:5 AMP

It seems my child always comes up short, Lord. He almost makes the team. . .then doesn't. He almost gets an A on a test. . .but makes a B instead. He tries out for the Christmas play at church, but doesn't get the part he wants. He gets the short end of the stick a lot, but there's one area where he never comes up short, and I'm so grateful! This verse reminds me that he will never have a deficit in wisdom as long as he asks You for more. You give it liberally, without pointing out the areas where he's fallen short. Thank You, Lord, for Your generosity. Amen.

Leaning on Jesus

*He who leans on, trusts in, and is confident of his own mind
and heart is a [self-confident] fool, but he who walks
in skillful and godly Wisdom shall be delivered.*
PROVERBS 28:26 AMP

Lord, my child is inundated with messages from friends, television, and movies, telling him that he has the power within himself to become all he wants to be. I want him to know that all wisdom comes from You. May his confidence be in You, Father, not Himself, not his own abilities. Sure, You've gifted him, but those gifts flow from Your throne, nowhere else. When he leans on You, trusts in You, and is confident in Your abilities (as opposed to his own), he is walking in godly wisdom. I love it, Lord! Amen.

Psalms, Hymns, and Spiritual Songs

*Let the message of Christ dwell among you richly as you teach
and admonish one another with all wisdom through psalms, hymns,
and songs from the Spirit, singing to God with gratitude in your hearts.*
COLOSSIANS 3:16 NIV

What a cool way to "get" wise, Lord. . .by admonishing one another
with psalms, hymns, and spiritual songs. As we greet one another with
praise, a song on our lips, wisdom follows. I love it! Thank You for
placing Your song in my child's life so that she can share it with friends
and encourage them as well. With gratitude in our hearts, our family
lifts a song of praise, Lord. Wisdom follows a happy heart, and that's
just what we long for today. Amen.

CHAPTER SIXTEEN

Hard Work/Diligence

—

Some of us are workaholics by nature. We go, go, go around the clock. Others need a little nudge just to get out of bed in the morning. Still others play the role of "nudger" (encouraging those who don't stick to their tasks). Where do you fit, parents? Are you a go-getter or the "wish I could go back to bed" type? Wherever you fit, you surely appreciate the need for hard work and diligence. It's critical to our survival. As adults we've learned this difficult lesson: if we don't work, we don't pay the bills. It's that simple. . .and that hard.

We are called by God to be diligent. A diligent person is persistent. He's careful. He refuses to give up, no matter how hard things get. As the old saying goes, "When the going gets tough, the tough get going" (Joseph Kennedy). A diligent person pushes back the covers and climbs out of bed, even when he wants to go on snoring. A diligent person fixes school lunches, makes sure the car is gassed up, and gets the bills paid on time.

Our children are watching how we respond to our workload. We need to teach them to keep going, even when the going gets tough. No, we won't always feel like it. Yes, we must. . . even when we feel we can't. Our kiddos need to keep going in school. Keep going in their relationships. Keep going when they have hard tasks ahead of them. They need to keep going when school projects loom, keep going when the bedroom needs to be cleaned, and keep going when Mom asks for help in the kitchen. Just like us, they need to move forward, even when they're completely convinced they can't. If we can convince them of this fact, their persistence will have a payoff. They will eventually reach their goals if they don't give up.

So, how do we teach our children to keep going? As with all things, by example. Beyond that, we have to pray for tenacity. Diligence. To be diligent means you put your nose to the grindstone and do whatever needs to be done. You don't just start the task; you finish it, not half-heartedly, but with whipped cream and a cherry on top.

It's time to pray, parents. Let's hit our knees, day in and day out, ever diligent. May this be our prayer as we lift our children before His throne: "Lord, we want to be a people who finish well. Amen."

All Things

I can do everything through
him who gives me strength.
PHILIPPIANS 4:13 NIV

Oh, how I love the word, "everything," Lord. I'm glad Your Word doesn't say that I can do *some* things or a *few* things. I can do *everything*. Please help me share this message with my child, Father. He doesn't feel like he can do all things. In fact, he's pretty hard on himself at times. If I can get him to grab hold of this "all things" mentality, it will change his life, especially once he realizes that You are happy to give him the strength to do it. Thank You for that, Lord. Amen.

When He Is Old

Train up a child in the way he should go,
even when he is old he will not depart from it.
PROVERBS 22:6 NASB

Raising a child is hard work, Lord! I'm not telling You anything You don't already know, but it's a day-in, day-out task, and sometimes I wonder if I'm up for it. I ask for Your help today, Father, to remain diligent in my attempts. My diligence will pay off when he's older, Lord. I have a promise in this verse that he will not depart from Your way if I train him up in the way he should go. The payoff is going to be great, Lord! Please remind me of that when I feel I can't go on. Thank You! Amen.

Leaving an Impression

These commandments that I give you today are to be on your hearts.
Impress them on your children. Talk about them when you sit at home and
when you walk along the road, when you lie down and when you get up.
Tie them as symbols on your hands and bind them on your foreheads.
Write them on the doorframes of your houses and on your gates.
DEUTERONOMY 6:6–9 NIV

I need to be diligent when it comes to teaching my children Your commands, Father. It's more than just a list of dos and don'ts. Your commands bring life. As we go about our daily lives, give me opportunities to share Your Word. May it become as much as part of their lives as breathing itself. Your Word is life, Father. I praise You for that life. Amen.

Willing to Work

For even when we were with you, we would give you this command:
If anyone is not willing to work, let him not eat. For we hear that
some among you walk in idleness, not busy at work, but busybodies.
Now such persons we command and encourage in the Lord Jesus
Christ to do their work quietly and to earn their own living.
2 THESSALONIANS 3:10–12 ESV

Ouch, Lord! What a tough verse. If a man won't work, he can't eat. I'll have to share that one with my child right away! Many times she doesn't want to cooperate, doesn't want to do her chores, her homework, or the dishes. May she grab on to the vision that Your commands bring life, and her diligence and hard work will have a lovely payoff— dinner! May she be encouraged to work hard, not out of frustration or obligation, but to please You. Amen.

Diligent Workers

The men in charge of the work were diligent,
and the repairs progressed under them. They rebuilt the temple
of God according to its original design and reinforced it.
2 CHRONICLES 24:13 NIV

You have a long history of choosing diligent workers, Lord. What a great example they've set for us. I'm so glad I have these Bible stories to refer to, for my child's sake as well as my own. When I see how hard they worked, it makes my tasks seem doable. I know my child's faith will be bolstered when he sees how long it took Nehemiah to build the wall. How hard Noah worked to build the ark. How long the Israelites traveled in the wilderness before reaching the Promised Land. Diligence has a payoff, and it's a great one! Amen.

The Riches of the Hunt

The lazy do not roast any game,
but the diligent feed on the riches of the hunt.
PROVERBS 12:27 NIV

What a fascinating picture of diligence, Lord! The perfect message, wrapped up in one little sentence. The lazy don't get to roast any game (no dinner for you!), but the hard-working, diligent folks get the best of the best. They feed on the riches of the hunt. Talk about a feast! I can't wait to share this message with my child. He will appreciate this analogy, especially the hunting parts! I pray he'll catch the vision and learn to work hard, Lord. Amen.

Progress Report

Give your complete attention to these matters.
Throw yourself into your tasks so that everyone
will see your progress.
1 TIMOTHY 4:15 NLT

This verse reminds me of the progress charts I used to get in school, Lord. My parents would look at them and either nod and smile (and give me pats on the back) or shake their heads and groan. You've given us tasks to do on this earth, Father. You've also given tasks to my children. May they throw themselves into those God-ordained tasks in such a way that their friends, their teachers, and their peers will all sit up and take notice. What a lovely progress report they will have! Amen.

It's Not Always Easy

But Moses said to the LORD, "Oh, my Lord, I am not eloquent,
either in the past or since you have spoken to your servant,
but I am slow of speech and of tongue." Then the LORD said to him,
"Who has made man's mouth? Who makes him mute, or deaf,
or seeing, or blind? Is it not I, the LORD? Now therefore go,
and I will be with your mouth and teach you what you shall speak."
EXODUS 4:10–12 ESV

How hard Moses must've worked to stand before the people and speak. I feel for him, Lord. It boggles my mind to think that You chose a man with a speech problem to lead Your people out of Israel. Wow! He worked hard—very hard—and accomplished the tasks You put in front of him. My child faces hard things, too. Some of them are so difficult he wants to give up. Thank You for this story of Moses, Lord, a true story of diligence. I can't wait to share it with my son.

Poverty-free

All hard work brings a profit, but mere talk leads only to poverty.
PROVERBS 14:23 NIV

It's one thing to talk about working, another thing to do it. That's why I'm so intrigued by this verse, Lord. I will profit if I keep my hand to the plow, but will be poverty-stricken if I stand around talking. I confess that I'm often guilty of this. I plan to work, but then don't follow through. My child is learning from my example. She plans to clean her room, and then doesn't. She plans to organize her closet, but doesn't follow through. Oops. I might have a little something to do with that one, Lord. Help me to train her by doing what I've said I will do. I'm going to need Your help for sure, Father! Amen.

Who's the Boss?

Work willingly at whatever you do, as though you were working for the Lord rather than for people. Remember that the Lord will give you an inheritance as your reward, and that the Master you are serving is Christ.
COLOSSIANS 3:23–24 NLT

I love it, Lord! You're the ultimate boss. Sure, we have earthly bosses. Yes, my child has "bosses," too (his parents, teachers, coaches, and so forth), but the person he really aims to please is You. Thanks for that reminder, Father. When he works for You, then You give him an inheritance as his reward. What a loving Master You are! Amen.

No Dozing on the Job

A little sleep, a little slumber, a little folding of the hands to rest—
and poverty will come on you like a thief and scarcity like an armed man.
PROVERBS 6:10–11 NIV

Sometimes we get a little lazy, Lord. We're not diligent. We don't carry through. When we give up on our work, things pile up around us. The house is a mess. The bills don't get paid. The clothes don't get washed. I see my child struggling with this sometimes. He lets things pile up. Thank You for this reminder that we must be diligent. If we take too much time to rest, the piles might just grow sky-high! Time to get back to work, Lord! Amen.

No Grumbling Allowed!

Do everything without grumbling or arguing, so that you may become
blameless and pure, "children of God without fault in a warped and
crooked generation." Then you will shine among them like stars in the sky.
PHILIPPIANS 2:14–15 NIV

Okay, I admit it, Lord. I do my work, but I grumble. Sometimes I grumble a lot. Because she's seen me grumble, my child grumbles, too. She can't seem to stay on task without griping and complaining. Oops. She's learned from the master. Help us both to lay aside our complaining and get to work. There will be a payoff for our diligence, but our hearts have to be in the right place. I know You can help us with this, Father, so I lay this request at Your feet. Amen.

Fruit Bearers

You did not choose me, but I chose you and appointed you so
that you might go and bear fruit—fruit that will last—
and so that whatever you ask in my name the Father will give you.
JOHN 15:16 NIV

It takes a long time for a tree to bear fruit, Lord. We're called to be fruit-bearers, too, and it seems to be taking a long time for some of it to appear in my life. I want to be effective for the Kingdom, Lord, and want my child to be effective, too. May he bear fruit (love, joy, peace, patience, and so on) that will serve as a testimony to others. If that fruit doesn't appear overnight, help us both to be as patient with one another as You are with us. Amen.

CHAPTER SEVENTEEN

Trust

———

Have you ever considered the idea that trust is a habit? When you're "out of the habit," you forget to trust. When you're "in the habit," it comes naturally. If you've ever struggled with trust issues in your own life, you can imagine what your child goes through at times. The stresses of trying to manage things on your own (in and "out of the habit" state) can be taxing, at best.

God wants us to trust Him. We know this. We read it in His Word. Yet knowing it and doing it are two completely different things. To trust means we totally let go of the situation and place it into His hands. It means we stop trying to fix things on our own. How easy this sounds. How difficult it is.

Why are we so afraid to trust? Perhaps it's because we're not yet convinced that God is for us, not against us. Maybe we're afraid of letting our guard down and then being hurt. We've been hurt in the past and don't like the feeling, thank you very much. So we choose to hang tight to the problem, convinced we can somehow fix it, or at least make things better on our own.

Without the Lord's help, we're incapable of overcoming the situations we face. He wants us to take His hand, to take Him at His word, and to keep moving forward, even when we're afraid. He's not interested in seeing us try to take the reins away from Him (though that's our tendency at times). He's definitely not keen on us bossing Him around. To trust means He gets to sit on the throne of our lives. We don't try to knock Him off of it when tough situations arise. It means our confidence is in Him, and Him, alone. Not in ourselves. Not in our abilities.

What does this have to do with our children? Everything. They're being taught (in school, on television, in the movies) to place their trust squarely in themselves. This message is prevalent. As adults, we know the consequences of this. . .disaster!

We need to get "in the habit" of trusting the Lord. When we do, our children will follow our lead and make it a habit, too. Before long, trusting Him will be second nature. We won't look inside ourselves for answers. . .we'll look to Him.

Perhaps the great Corrie ten Boom said it best: "Never be afraid to trust an unknown future to a known God." Amen, Corrie. Amen.

Present Your Requests

Do not be anxious about anything, but in every situation,
by prayer and petition, with thanksgiving, present your requests to God.
PHILIPPIANS 4:6 NIV

Be anxious for nothing. Sounds impossible, Lord! That's why we need You so much. On our own, we just couldn't do it. I know that my child struggles with anxiety. She's probably picked up on some of that from me. To really teach her to trust, I must completely hand over all of my problems to You, Father. I start today by emptying my hands of the things that have me stressed out at this very moment. Please calm my heart, Lord, so that I can be free from anxiety. Help me to guide my child, so she can live a trust-filled life. Amen.

Not My Own

Trust in the LORD with all your heart and do not lean on
your own understanding; in all your ways submit to Him,
and He will make your paths straight.
PROVERBS 3:5–6 NIV

I get into trouble whenever I start to lean on my own understanding, Lord. Instead of trusting You completely, I try to figure it out. If I'm short on finances, I try to come up with a solution. If I'm in over my head at work, I try to fix it. I see some of these same "fix it" traits in my child. He's a go-getter, always wanting to fix, fix, fix. I need to teach him to trust, trust, trust. . .not in himself, but You. Can You help me with that today, Lord? Amen.

Trusting in the Rock

The LORD is my rock, my fortress and my deliverer;
my God is my rock, in whom I take refuge,
my shield and the horn of my salvation, my stronghold.
PSALM 18:2 NIV

Everything is so shaky, Lord. We can't put our trust in anything anymore. I've watched my child try! So many times she thinks she's on steady ground, but then a spiritual earthquake comes. Help me to teach her that You are our Rock, Lord. You are steady when nothing else is. When things around us are crumbling, You hold firm. We can hold fast to You, Father. Thank You for that promise. Amen.

A Mighty Fortress

I will say of the LORD, "He is my refuge
and my fortress, my God, in whom I trust."
PSALM 91:2 NIV

Oh, how I want to protect my child! I want to wrap him in my arms and hide him away from all of the bad things out there in this big, wide world. I know this is impossible, of course, but the temptation is there, all the same. That's why I'm so glad to read in Your Word that You are our fortress. You hem us in on every side, protecting us from our enemies. You do a far better job than I could ever do, Lord. I put my trust in You, my child's ultimate refuge! Amen.

Learning to Trust

Trust in him at all times, O people;
pour out your heart before him; God is a refuge for us.
PSALM 62:8 ESV

Learning to trust is a process. I know this from my own spiritual journey. To fully trust means you can "let go and let God" as the old saying goes. We can only let go of something if we genuinely trust the One into whose hands we're placing it. You are trustworthy, Father! May my child learn this amazing lesson so that she can begin to let go of some of the things she's held on to. May she pour out her heart before You and take refuge in You, O Lord. Amen.

Help Is Coming

Commit everything you do to the LORD.
Trust him, and he will help you.
PSALM 37:5 NLT

Sometimes my child stands back when he's afraid, hoping someone else will sweep in and rescue him. That's one reason I love this verse so much, Lord. When we commit everything we do to You, when we place our trust wholly in the work You've done on Calvary, You truly will sweep in and help us when we're in need. I can't wait to tell my child that help is on the way. All he has to do is trust. . .and then call out to You. Thank You for being our helper, Lord. Amen.

The Eternal Rock

Trust in the LORD forever, for the LORD,
the LORD himself, is the Rock eternal.
ISAIAH 26:4 NIV

I love the word *eternal*, Lord. It boggles my mind to think that life will go on long after we've passed on. Your eternal plan is difficult for an adult to comprehend, and even harder for a child. Help me to convey "eternity" to my child so that she can rest in the assurance that she will have everlasting life. You—O, Rock eternal—will be at the center of it all, for we have placed our trust in You. What comfort. What joy! Amen.

Mere Mortals

In God, whose word I praise—in God I trust and
am not afraid. What can mere mortals do to me?
PSALM 56:4 NIV

When we trust in You we don't have to be afraid, Lord. We lift high our voices, singing praise in the middle of the battle, never once giving thought to worry. Okay, so maybe we worry a little, but You're right there, to remind us that "mere mortals" (any enemies who rise up against us) can't possibly harm us when You're on our side. May my child learn this lesson at an early age so he doesn't fear "mere mortals." As long as he places his trust in You, he has nothing—and no one—to fear. Amen!

My Salvation

"Surely God is my salvation; I will trust and not be afraid. The LORD, the LORD himself, is my strength and my defense; he has become my salvation."
ISAIAH 12:2 NIV

What a wonderful word: *salvation*. You've saved us from so many things, Father—our sin, our pain, our past. When we put our trust in You, we don't have to live in fear. I want my child to see this promise firsthand. Please remind her that You are her defense. You are her salvation—the One who has delivered her from destruction. What an amazing God You are! Amen.

Trustworthy Words

Sovereign Lord, you are God! Your covenant is trustworthy, and you have promised these good things to your servant.
2 SAMUEL 7:28 NIV

To place your trust in someone, you have to believe what they say. Today I pray that my child will learn to place his trust in Your Word. Every word in the Bible is true. We can depend on it. When my child is struggling, remind him that there are answers for every problem in the Bible. The words written there are trustworthy. They won't fail. They are a promise, not just for my children, but for future generations. Thank You for Your unfailing Word, Lord! I know we can count on You. Amen.

Never Forsaken

Those who know your name trust in you, for you,
Lord, have never forsaken those who seek you.
PSALM 9:10 NIV

"Never forsaken." I have to pause for breath as I read those words, Father. I've felt abandoned by people many times over. It feels so good to know You won't ever leave me. My child has experienced those "forsaken" feelings at times, too. She's struggled with feelings of abandonment. Whisper to her heart today, I pray. Remind her that You will never forsake her, as long as she seeks You and puts her trust in You. What a faithful Father You are! Amen.

When I Am Afraid

When I am afraid, I put my trust in you.
PSALM 56:3 NIV

Sometimes we just want to crouch under the covers, Lord. The world is a scary place. We get hurt and then cower in fear. What joy, to read that we can turn to You when we're afraid. You are always there (even under the covers). You know our hearts. You can deliver us from fear. Today I ask that You comfort my child and remove any fears he might be facing. Replace fear with trust. Then pull back the covers and show him that he truly can face any obstacles with his hand in Yours. Amen.

Properly Placed Trust

Those who trust in their riches will fall,
but the righteous will thrive like a green leaf.
PROVERBS 11:28 NIV

My child is picking up on all sorts of messages from television, movies, and music, Lord. She's even learning some not-so-great things from friends. They are tugging at her heart, asking her to place her trust in a wide variety of things that simply won't prove trustworthy or true. When she's tempted to give in, to trust in the things of this world, remind her of this verse: whoever trusts in riches (earthly wealth or possessions) will fall. The righteous (the ones who place their trust solely in You) will thrive like green leaves. What a lovely image, Father. Amen.

I'm Blessed!

LORD Almighty, blessed is the one who trusts in you.
PSALM 84:12 NIV

I love this promise, Father! You will bless the man (or child) who trusts You. There's a payoff for trust. To walk in Your blessing means a life of favor. A life of security, as our heartbeat comes into sync with Yours. How wonderful that this blessing doesn't have any age barriers. You offer it to my children, and their children, and to all future generations, as long as we trust in You. Help me to share this message often, so that my family will be truly blessed. Amen.

CHAPTER EIGHTEEN

Health

—

It seems the busier we are, the more we struggle with health issues. This even spills over onto our kids. Crazy schedules, fast food, lack of sleep, too much time on the computer. . .and we're a mess! Our bodies were never meant to keep up with it all.

As we learn to pray for our child's health, we can't help but face the inevitable truth: we need to live more balanced lives. It's not enough to pray, "Lord, heal my child." We might also need to pray, "Please forgive me for letting him go day after day, week after week working too hard, sleeping too little." This isn't always the case, of course, but sometimes their little immune systems break down because they're overly exhausted.

Before we pray, let's look at a familiar scripture, (1 Corinthians 6:19–20 NIV): "Do you not know that your bodies are temples of the Holy Spirit, who is in you, whom you have received from God? You are not your own; you were bought at a price. Therefore honor God with your body."

Our bodies are temples. They are a habitation for the Holy Spirit, a place for God to reside. When we're not taking care of those bodies, we don't give Him a very good dwelling place, do we? Instead of being focused on Him, we're nursing our sick bodies back to health. What a distraction!

There are so many scriptures about health. Many will be covered in this chapter. Yet one stands out above all others—3 John 1:2 (NIV): "Dear friend, I pray that you may enjoy good health and that all may go well with you, even as your soul is getting along well."

God doesn't just want our bodies to be healthy; He wants our souls (our minds and hearts) to be healthy. When we're out of balance, this is impossible. When we bring our activity levels down and our prayer time up, it balances out.

So, how do we pray for our child's health? It's more than just shooting up popcorn prayers in the moment: "Help Johnny get over his cold." "Help Susie; she's really tired today and has a test." Dedicating ourselves to pray for our children's health means dedicating ourselves to their health. It means cutting back on the craziness and giving them proper nutrition. It means getting them to bed on time and making sure they wake up refreshed. Then, as we pray for their health, we pray with a clear conscience, knowing we've done our part.

Okay, okay. . .so this isn't as easy as it sounds. We have trouble taking care of our own bodies. We're called by God to do the best we can, so we have to make health more of a focus. Ready to give it a shot? Great! Let's spend some time making a list of things we can do to give our kids a healthier lifestyle, and then get busy praying.

Even as Your Soul Prospers

Dear friend, I pray that you may enjoy good health
and that all may go well with you,
even as your soul is getting along well.
3 JOHN 1:2 NIV

Lord, I love this scripture. You care about our health. We've had our struggles in that area at times, Lord, but You always come through for us. Thank You for the promise that my child can have health and healing. I also pray for her spiritual health. May her soul "get along well" as this scripture says. May her heart, mind, and body always be healthy and whole, Lord. May her spirit be strong as she links arms with You. Amen.

Healing to the Body

Do not be wise in your own eyes; fear the LORD and shun evil.
This will bring health to your body
and nourishment to your bones.
PROVERBS 3:7–8 NIV

So many times we do things that cause our health to suffer. We don't sleep. We eat the wrong foods. We work too hard. As I read this verse today I'm intrigued. How fascinating, to know that turning away from evil can actually be healing to my body. I pray this for my child, as well. As he turns from unhealthy friendships, from poor choices, from a stressful workload, You will bring refreshment to his bones. I'm so grateful for that, Lord. Amen.

Restored Health

Lord, your discipline is good, for it leads to life and health.
You restore my health and allow me to live!
ISAIAH 38:16 NLT

Discipline leads to life and health. I can't wait to share this one with my child, Lord! She's not always a fan of discipline. (Is any child?) Still, this verse should help. When she's open to being disciplined, You're freed up to give her health and life. I pray she can grab hold of this idea and respond by living in obedience so that she can walk in health all of her days. I praise You for giving her this choice, Lord. Amen.

Honeycomb

Gracious words are a honeycomb,
sweet to the soul and healing to the bones.
PROVERBS 16:24 NIV

Our words can impact our health. I've learned this firsthand, Lord. When we're worked up, spewing ugly words, it can affect us physically. When we offer sweet words—a honeycomb, as this scripture says— they actually mend us from the inside out. Our gentle, sweet words don't just soothe our hearts and minds; they provide healing to our souls and even our bones. I can't wait to pass this on to my child, Lord. May his words be sweet, so that he can enjoy long life and health. Amen.

A Healing Word

*Then they cried to the LORD in their trouble, and he saved them
from their distress. He sent out his word and healed them;
he rescued them from the grave. Let them give thanks to the LORD
for his unfailing love and his wonderful deeds for mankind.*
PSALM 107:19–21 NIV

How many times have I heard my child cry out over the years, Lord?
There have been quite a few tears along the way. I'm so grateful for
today's verse because it reminds me that You hear our cries. You save
us from our distresses. Best of all, You send Your Word and heal us. I
love that picture, Father. Your Word—spoken over us—brings healing. Even though we can't reach out and touch You, we have Your
Word. We simply open the Bible and read the words written there and
receive healing.

Healing Benefits

*Praise the LORD, my soul, and forget not all his benefits—
who forgives all your sins and heals all your diseases, who redeems
your life from the pit and crowns you with love and compassion.*
PSALM 103:2–4 NIV

What wonderful benefits there are to loving You, Lord. . . You forgive
our sins and You heal our diseases. You redeem us and crown us with
love and compassion. This gives me great hope as I place my child into
Your hands. You love her even more than I do, Father. You long to give
her every benefit of the Kingdom—from salvation to healing to complete restoration. You're a gracious God, so generous to Your children.
Praise You for that. Amen.

A Life Preserved

*The Lord protects and preserves them—they are counted among the blessed
in the land—he does not give them over to the desire of their foes.
The Lord sustains them on their sickbed
and restores them from their bed of illness.*
PSALM 41:2–3 NIV

My child has a long life ahead of him, Lord. That's why I want him to
stay healthy. He has quite a road in front of him and poor health could
get in the way. Thank You for the promise in this scripture. I'm so glad
You will protect him and preserve his life. You care very much about
every aspect of his life, even the times when he's under the covers,
running a fever or displaying other symptoms of illness. Thank You for
raising him up, time and time again. I'm truly grateful. Amen.

One Touch

*They came to Bethsaida, and some people brought
a blind man and begged Jesus to touch him.*
MARK 8:22 NIV

I love the stories of Jesus healing the sick because they let me know
just how much You care about hurting, wounded people, Lord. You
love us enough to stop everything You're doing just to whisper "Peace,
be still." You care so much that You intervene and turns things around.
As I read this story to my child today, bolster her faith. May she come
to see that one touch from You can heal her from the inside out. Amen.

Healing of the Heart

He heals the brokenhearted and binds up their wounds.
PSALM 147:3 NIV

Healing involves far more than the physical body, Lord. This I know from my own life. Many times our hearts are broken and need mending. You're perfectly capable of healing them and binding up our internal wounds, as well as external ones. Today I ask You to bind any wounds in my child's heart. If there are hidden pains, hurts of betrayals, I pray he will let go of them and receive Your healing. Wrap Your arms around him, Father, and bring complete healing, I pray. Amen.

And I Will Be Healed

Heal me, LORD, and I will be healed;
save me and I will be saved,
for you are the one I praise.
JEREMIAH 17:14 NIV

There's such confidence in this verse. "Heal me and I will be healed." There's no doubt in those words. When we place our trust in God, we can't waffle back and forth in our faith. Either we believe He's going to follow through, or we don't. I pray for my child's confidence level today, Father. Boost his faith. Increase his trust. May he speak with confidence as he tells others about the great works You are doing in his life. Amen.

CHAPTER NINETEEN

Uniqueness

---

f you look up the word *unique* you'll find a couple of intriguing definitions:

1. existing as the only one or as the sole example; single; solitary in type or characteristics
2. having no like or equal; unparalleled; incomparable

What wonderful definitions! We are all part of the body of Christ, all created in His image, but completely unique! We exist (each one of us) as a sole example. There's no one like us, no matter how far we search. There is no "like," no equal. We are unparalleled and incomparable.

Wow! That really puts a positive spin on it, doesn't it? God never intended for us to be like everyone else. Of course, this raises an obvious question: How is it possible to be a believer (part of the family) and yet completely different from our brothers and sisters? If you think about the human body, the hand doesn't look like the foot. The leg doesn't look like the shoulder. Each part is completely unique to the other, but they all work together. That's how it is in the body of Christ. We were never meant to be cookie-cutter Christians. How boring that would be! We're called to be set apart, with different gifts, different personalities, and different perspectives. In this case, "different" is good. Very, very good, in fact.

Why, then, do our children try so hard to be like everyone

else? They want to look like their friends, act like their friends, and so on. It's because they're afraid to embrace their individuality. They want to fit in (sometimes at any cost).

That's where you come in, parents. So what if our kids aren't like some of the others? So what if their gifts and abilities are different? In God's eyes, they're beautiful members of the family! You can pray for your child to accept her differences, to enjoy her uniqueness. You can pray that she sees herself as usable and loveable. You can pray that God would touch her heart and help her see that she doesn't have to fit in with the crowd; she already fits in with Him. Most of all, you can pray that she will learn to praise God for creating her just the way she is.

Ready to get to it? Dive right in, in your own unique way!

Embrace It!

Every good and perfect gift is from above, coming down from the Father of the heavenly lights, who does not change like shifting shadows.
JAMES 1:17 NIV

What is it about kids that makes them want to dress alike, talk alike, and act alike, Lord? As hard as I try, my kiddos rarely embrace their own uniqueness. That's my prayer today, that they would see themselves as rare jewels, precious and unique, but gloriously beautiful and precious to You. Help them to lay down the desire to follow after others, to be like their peers. Embracing their uniqueness means they're taking hold of the gift of being created in Your image. Thank You for nudging them in this area, Father. I'm so grateful. Amen.

And It Was Good

And God saw everything that he had made, and behold, it was very good. And there was evening and there was morning, the sixth day.
GENESIS 1:31 ESV

Everything You created is good, Father. What a remarkable thought! That means that I—Your creation—am good. My child is good, too. That doesn't mean she always behaves herself or acts in a rational way, but she's good in Your eyes. You made her exactly the way You wanted her to be made—with the right hair, eyes, physique. Sure, she's not always happy with how she looks (what woman is?), but I ask You today to convince her that she's deliberately unique and set apart for great things. Thank You for that reminder in my own life, too! Amen.

Fan into Flame

For this reason I remind you to fan into flame the gift of God,
which is in you through the laying on of my hands.
2 TIMOTHY 1:6 NIV

My gifts are unique to me, Lord. No one sings like I do, or writes like I do, and so on. You made me this way on purpose. . .different from the rest. The same is true with my child. His talents and abilities are unique to him. I'm so glad, too! No cookie cutters in our family, Lord! He's his own kid, completely unique and individual. Because he's created in the image of a very creative God, I can rest easy in the fact that his differences are what make him special. Thank You for that reminder today. Amen.

Wonderful Are Your Works

I praise you, for I am fearfully and wonderfully made.
Wonderful are your works; my soul knows it very well.
PSALM 139:14 ESV

You didn't mess up when You made me, Lord. I wasn't a mistake. All of interesting quirks aren't just freak accidents. . .they're a special design that You took Your time with. I'm so glad to know this. I'm also glad for my child's sake. Sometimes she frowns on her differences. She doesn't want to embrace her uniqueness. Help me show her to-day that nothing is a mistake—nothing in her physical appearance and nothing in her personality. She is one of Your many wonderful works, Lord, and I adore her, every quirky detail! Amen.

The Apple of His Eye

For this is what the LORD Almighty says: "After the Glorious
One has sent me against the nations that have plundered you—
for whoever touches you touches the apple of his eye."
ZECHARIAH 2:8 NIV

It's so interesting to think about how many kids You have, Lord. Billions of them, all over this globe! Our family belongs to a huge, vast family with brothers and sisters we'll never even meet in person. In the midst of all of that, You look at each of us as individuals, and say, "You're the apple of my eye." You play favorites. I'm Your favorite. My child is Your favorite. We're all Your favorite! Today, remind me of that principle. May each of my children be the apple of my eye, Lord, even the ones who are a little on the naughty side. Amen.

※

His Treasured Possession

For you are a people holy to the LORD your God. The LORD
your God has chosen you out of all the peoples on the face
of the earth to be his people, his treasured possession.
DEUTERONOMY 7:6 NIV

You cherish us, Lord. The reminder in today's verse brings a big smile to my face. I know what it's like to treasure my child, Father. She means the world to me. I would do anything for her. Thank You for making all of us Your treasures. Show me how to treat my child as a gift, one that brings delight with every new discovery. I'm so grateful for my little treasure, Lord. Thank You for entrusting her to me. Amen.

Count Those Hairs!

But even the hairs of your head are all numbered.
MATTHEW 10:30 ESV

We're all so different in appearance, Lord. Keeping up with us must be quite a challenge. It boggles my mind to read that You know how many hairs are on our heads. Wow. I can't keep up with my child's socks, let alone his hair. It's just too much! Yet You're in the details, Father, even the ones that elude me. Thank You for caring enough about my kiddo to know what makes him tick. Because I know You're in the details, I can rest easy, Lord. Amen.

Our Crazy Schedules

You have searched me, LORD, and you know me. You know when
I sit and when I rise; you perceive my thoughts from afar.
You discern my going out and my lying down;
you are familiar with all my ways.
PSALM 139:1–3 NIV

We don't just look different, Lord. . .we are different. We have different personalities, different schedules, and different interests. I don't know how You keep up with it all! I have a hard time with my kiddos. Whew! Talk about a crazy schedule. It's fascinating to think that You're familiar with all our ways. You know when we sit and when we lie down. You know when it's time to leave for soccer practice and when we're headed off to church. You know when my kiddo is brushing her teeth for bed and when she's snoozing. What a miraculous God You are! Amen.

A Royal Priesthood

But you are a chosen people, a royal priesthood, a holy nation,
God's special possession, that you may declare the praises of
him who called you out of darkness into his wonderful light.
1 PETER 2:9 NIV

Wow, Lord! We're a royal priesthood! We're a "set apart" people group because we've given our hearts to You. I love that idea. My child is part of that "royal" family, and he's been called out of darkness into Your marvelous light. May he take on his role of priest with fervor, singing Your praises to all with whom he comes in contact. Thank You for the privilege of being one of Your own, Lord. Amen.

Members Individually

Now you are Christ's body, and individually members of it.
1 CORINTHIANS 12:27 NASB

I see those really large families on TV, Lord, and I wonder how they do it. I can hardly keep up with my own crew! Keeping up with each of the kids and remembering that they're individuals takes up a lot of time. (Frankly, I don't know how You do it with all of Your kids.) When You look down on us, You don't see us as one and the same. You see distinct individuals, each with his own purpose and calling. When You see my children, they are each unique with different callings and gifts. Thank You for seeing us individually, Father! Amen.

No Inferiority Complex

Indeed, I consider that I am not in the
least inferior to these super-apostles.
2 CORINTHIANS 11:5 ESV

Even the apostles wondered where—or how—they fit together at
times, Lord. They were all different, one from the other, and yet they
all knew that their calling was secure. They recognized their uniqueness as a gift. That's my prayer for my child today. May she recognize
her uniqueness as a gift and say with confidence (as the apostles did),
"I am not the least inferior." Amen.

The Hope of My Calling

There is one body and one Spirit, just as also you were called
in one hope of your calling; one Lord, one faith, one baptism,
one God and Father of all who is over all and through all and in all.
EPHESIANS 4:4–6 NASB

I love the family of God, in part because of the diversity among its
members. I love the diversity in my family, too. Each member is unique.
It's so fascinating to think that, in spite of all of the diversity, there's
only one body, one Spirit, one Lord, one faith, one baptism. Just one. I
know why, though. It's because (as we've told our kids so many times)
"When God created you, He broke the mold." It's really true in Your
case, Lord. There is no need for other gods because You are all we will
ever need. Our faith in You is the only faith we will ever need. What a
wonderful reminder in this special verse. Amen.

No One Like You

*"There is no one holy like the LORD;
there is no one besides you; there is no Rock like our God."*
1 SAMUEL 2:2 NIV

We are created in Your image, Lord, and what a unique image it is. This verse reminds us that there is no one like You, Father. No one is holy like You. No one loves like You do. There is no other Rock like You. You created us in Your image, Father. I'm just figuring out that part of the reason we're all different is because there are so many different facets to You, our creative Creator. You want us to celebrate our uniqueness. Today I choose to do that. . .for me and my child. Amen.

One in You

*There is neither Jew nor Greek, there is neither slave nor free,
there is no male and female, for you are all one in Christ Jesus.*
GALATIANS 3:28 ESV

How fascinating, Lord! We're individuals with our own unique quirks, but we are all one in You. That means that my child is part of a greater whole. He is bonded with every other member in the body of Christ. He fits in, even with his unique ways of doing things. You've "fitted" him together with the other members of Your body in a special way so that he can impact his world. Thank You for making us one, Lord. What a blessed family we are. Amen.

CHAPTER TWENTY

Future Spouse

When our kids are little, we don't want to think about whom they will marry. In fact, we cringe at the idea of letting them drive a car or go on a date, let alone get married! By the time they're in junior high, many of them are facing peer pressure. The whole boyfriend/girlfriend topic usually comes up during this season. We know that they are years away from marriage (and God's best for them), so how can we pray during the formative years? Do we hide them away from the opposite sex? Put our foot down? Do we guard who they spend time with or what they do with their peers? Do we—hard as it might be—think ahead to the time when our child will be married?

No matter your child's age, it's not too soon to begin praying for his future spouse. Think about that for a moment. Even if he's very young, God already knows whom he will marry. . .and when. He knows how many children they will have and what those children will be like. As parents, we have an obligation to pray for that young woman, even now. Pray for her safety. Pray that she would remain pure. Pray that she would grow strong in the Lord, and that her heart would be prepared for your son, when the time comes.

Sure, this goes against everything we want to think about during our child's formative years, but God will honor those prayers. He'll do something else, too. He will begin to soften your heart toward that future daughter-in-law. He will give you a deep, precious love for her.

So, how do we begin? We don't even know this person, after all. Start by praying for her walk with the Lord, that she would come to Him at an early age and never walk away. Pray that she would be a lover of people, as well as a lover of God. Pray for her heart and for her purity. Pray for her protection as she grows, that nothing would harm her. Pray for attributes like patience, loyalty, commitment.

In short, pray for her as you would pray for your own child. One day she will be, you know. You'd better start getting used to the idea now. She needs your covering as much as your kiddos do, so don't hold back any longer, even if the idea of one day becoming an in-law makes you cringe.

You can do this. When the time comes—when you meet her face to face and see the lovely woman staring back at you— you will be glad you did.

A Beautiful Heart

I will give you a new heart and put a new spirit in you;
I will remove from you your heart of stone and give you a heart of flesh.
EZEKIEL 36:26 NIV

Lord, I pray for my child's future spouse today. May she have a beautiful heart. Above all external beauty, I long for my son to marry a woman who's beautiful from the inside out. Begin to work on softening her heart now, taking away any "stone" parts and replacing them with a heart of flesh. Prepare her for my son, Lord, and make her heart ready by whispering in her ear, telling her that You adore her. Amen.

Lover of People

No one has ever seen God; but if we love one another,
God lives in us and his love is made complete in us.
1 JOHN 4:12 NIV

Lord, I pray that my child's future spouse will be a lover of people. May he treat her like the princess she is, but may he also love and care about others, as well. Give him a heart for people who are hurting. Give him a passion for the lost. Give him a desire to make a difference in his community. Give him zeal for people across the globe who need to hear the Gospel, and for people next door, as well. Thank You for the call on his life, Lord. Amen.

Lover of God

I love the LORD, for he heard my voice;
he heard my cry for mercy.
PSALM 116:1 NIV

Above all, Father, I pray that my child's future spouse has a solid relationship with You. May she fall in love with You so wholly, so completely, that it transforms every area of her life. May she turn to You, and You alone, when her heart is aching. I pray that she recognizes Your whispers, responds to Your nudges, and celebrates Your presence. Together, my child and his spouse will be a powerful duo! Amen.

The Narrow Gate

"Enter by the narrow gate. For the gate is wide and the way
is easy that leads to destruction, and those who enter by it are many.
For the gate is narrow and the way is hard that leads to life,
and those who find it are few."
MATTHEW 7:13–14 ESV

The world is filled with people walking a wide path. They don't even realize they're off course, Lord. My child's future spouse is set apart, called to reach those on the wide path and help them make a better choice. I know she will encounter negativity and possibly hostility as she shares the message of the Gospel, Lord, so protect her, I pray. Give her courage to go along with the call You've placed on her life, but also give her the ability to pick up the pieces and move forward when people don't respond as she hopes. Amen.

Prayer for Patience

You too, be patient and stand firm,
because the Lord's coming is near.
JAMES 5:8 NIV

Lord, I hate to admit it, but my child's future spouse is going to have to be very patient. She's going to have to muddle through some of my kiddo's interesting personality quirks. Begin to prepare her now for the fact that her husband is going to be unique, different, and maybe even a little quirky. May she find these traits endearing, Lord, I pray. While you're at it, please work on my child's patience, too. Sometimes he needs an extra dose. Amen.

Prayer for Loyalty

Their hearts were not loyal to him,
they were not faithful to his covenant.
PSALM 78:37 NIV

I pray that my child's future spouse would be a loyal person, Lord, someone with stick-to-itiveness. I pray that he won't give up easily or throw in the towel. Sometimes my child wants to give up, so she'll need someone who's willing to stay the course, no matter how difficult things get. Loyal hearts, faithful hearts, can make it through just about anything, as long as they beat in unison. Prepare these hearts today, I pray. Amen.

Prayer for Protection

But the Lord is faithful,
and he will strengthen you and protect you
from the evil one.
2 THESSALONIANS 3:3 NIV

Lord, I'm always praying for protection for my child, but sometimes forget to pray for his future spouse's protection. Guard her, I pray. Keep her safe. Protect her from the evil in this world. Give her peace instead of fear. Hem her in, behind and before. Remind her daily that walking close to You is the best possible guarantee for a safe, fulfilled life. Thank You for caring so much about her, Lord. Amen.

Prayer for Contentment

Not that I am speaking of being in need, for I have learned in whatever situation I am to be content. I know how to be brought low, and I know how to abound. In any and every circumstance, I have learned the secret of facing plenty and hunger, abundance and need.
PHILIPPIANS 4:11–12 ESV

We're all on a learning curve, Lord. I know I am, anyway. "Learning" to be content is a process; it doesn't happen overnight. That's why I'm asking now that You would begin to work on my child's future spouse. May he be a contented man, one who isn't always uneasy, wishing things were different. Settle his heart and make him content in You so that he can one day be content in marriage, work, and parenting. Amen.

Commitment

Commit your work to the LORD,
and your plans will be established.
PROVERBS 16:3 ESV

I pray that my child's future spouse will be committed—to their relationship, to her walk with the Lord, and to the body of Christ. Begin to work on her now, I pray, so that she's learned the necessary skills by the time she's married. Give her the ability to stay with childhood projects from start to finish, so that she learns the lesson of finishing well. Please work on my child in this area, too. Sometimes he starts things and doesn't finish them. He comes by it honestly, I suppose. Work on us all, I pray. Amen.

Transformed, Not Conformed

Do not conform to the pattern of this world, but be transformed
by the renewing of your mind. Then you will be able to test and
approve what God's will is—his good, pleasing and perfect will.
ROMANS 12:2 NIV

I've prayed this prayer so many times for my child, Father. She's had her moments of conforming when she should be transforming. I know it's difficult, especially with so many things tugging at her. I pray today for her future spouse, that he would be transformed (from his time spent with You) and not conformed (to the people/situations around him). If they're both transformed, what a powerful team they will be! Amen.

Godly Wisdom

If any of you lacks wisdom, you should ask God,
who gives generously to all without finding fault,
and it will be given to you.
JAMES 1:5 NIV

Lord, I pray today that my child's future spouse will be filled with Your wisdom. I'm not as concerned about how "smart" she is by the world's standards. Maybe she'll be highly educated; maybe not. Education without wisdom is pointless, so I pray for godly wisdom to flow. You don't hold back Your wisdom from those who ask, Father. What a wonderful promise. So, I'm asking on her behalf today. May she overflow with godly wisdom. Amen.

Prayer for Overcoming

"I have told you these things, so that in me you may have peace.
In this world you will have trouble. But take heart! I have overcome the world."
JOHN 16:33 NIV

Father, I pray for my child's future spouse to be an overcomer, someone who jumps over hurdles with ease. I know he will face challenges as he grows up. Everyone does. Every hurdle can be overcome if he walks with You. May he fly over those obstacles, Lord. May they not hinder him as he presses toward the goal. Give him the assurance to know that he's got the goods. He's an overcomer. Amen.

Godly Character

Not only so, but we also glory in our sufferings,
because we know that suffering produces perseverance;
perseverance, character; and character, hope.
ROMANS 5:3–4 NIV

It's hard to picture any child glorying in their sufferings, Lord. Yet I know that suffering causes us to persevere, and perseverance brings about godly character. I don't know what my child's future spouse is facing today, but whatever it is, please help her to persevere. May her perseverance pay off in the end as she grows into the amazing woman of God You've called her to be. Amen.

A Clear Path

You make known to me the path of life; you will fill me with
joy in your presence, with eternal pleasures at your right hand.
PSALM 16:11 NIV

I love this promise, Lord! You make known to us the path we're to take. As I think about my child's future spouse today, I'm reminded that You are even now making his path known. You're whispering "Go this way" or "Go that way" in his ear. I'm grateful that You care so much about each step of the journey. May the path be clear for all of us, I pray. Amen.

CHAPTER TWENTY-ONE

Answering the Call

———

What an amazing call God has put on each of our lives. When we're part of His family, we're not just there to take up space. We're there to make an impact in the world. Many times we sit back, hoping someone else will rise to the occasion so that we don't have to. What a shame! We need to start seeing our call as something we get to do, not something we have to do.

When you think about where your child fits into this conversation, where do your thoughts go? Do you say, "Oh, he's too young to start thinking about that" or "She's not really thinking about God-things just yet." It's never too early to talk about the fact that God has a unique, specific call for all of his kids, no matter their age.

Not convinced? Think about Timothy, a young man who made an impact in the early church. Think about Josiah, the youngest king to rule over Israel. Think about David, fighting the mighty Goliath when he was just a boy. Each of these people had a call, a destiny. Each stepped out in faith to answer the call.

Will your child answer the call? That depends, in part, on what you train him to do. If you encourage him to incline his ear toward God, to hear His voice and to respond in faith, then he's more likely to answer the call affirmatively. That's what you want, of course! God's plans for us are bigger than anything we can come up with. Why would we want to keep our children from walking the road He longs for them to walk?

How do we pray for our kiddos? We need to pray that they

seek God first, that they spend time in prayer, not just asking for things, but waiting on the Lord to hear His voice. (We might have to explain this concept to them. God truly speaks to the heart of His believers.) We need to pray that they recognize His voice and then step out in faith as ideas flow.

A child who recognizes the call on his life will keep his parents hopping. He'll sign up for mission trips, gather food items to donate to the food pantry, raise funds for those less fortunate. He'll be tuned in to the needs around him. So, let him do his thing, parents. He's learning how to listen and respond, and that's a very good thing. In fact, you might just learn a few things from him along the way.

It's time to pray for our children to hear the Lord's voice and to answer the call. Prep yourselves, parents! Your schedule is about to get busy!

Dedicated

"I prayed for this child, and the LORD answered my prayer and gave him to me. Now I give him back to the LORD. He will belong to the LORD all his life." And he worshiped the Lord there.
1 SAMUEL 1:27–28 NCV

I can relate to Hannah, the mother of Samuel. She prayed for a son, and You blessed her with a son, Lord. (What a blessing!) Then, while he was still young, Hannah dedicated him back to You. I know that You've placed a call on my child's life and I have to dedicate (give her back) to You so that she can grow to be the woman You've called her to be. I trust You, Father. May the call on her life be fulfilled, and may I stand back, a happy observer, as she steps out in faith, ready to answer the call. Amen.

Irrevocable

For the gifts and the calling of God are irrevocable.
ROMANS 11:29 NASB

Thank You for the call You've placed on my life, Father. I'm blessed when I think about all You've entrusted to me. I'm just as excited about the call on my child's life. She's got such a bright future and is ready to follow after You wholeheartedly. I'm so grateful Your gifts and calling are irrevocable. You won't change Your mind. You won't take them back. I can rest easy, knowing my child's future is secure in You. What a blessing, Father. Amen.

Job Done!

I have brought you glory on earth by
finishing the work you gave me to do.
JOHN 17:4 NIV

Oh Lord. . .how wonderful to be able to say, "Job done!" When we reach the end of this life, may we be able to look You in the eye and say, "I accomplished the tasks You gave me to do." I pray this for my child, too. You've given her much to do, and she's barely begun. So many years stretch out in front of her. May she truly glorify You during this window of time You've given her on planet Earth. May she be able to say, at the end of her days, "I did it, Lord! With Your help, I did what You called me to do." Amen.

Set Apart

While they were worshiping the Lord and fasting,
the Holy Spirit said, "Set apart for me Barnabas
and Saul for the work to which I have called them."
ACTS 13:2 NIV

As I think about this verse, I get so excited, Lord. You've called us. Chosen us. Set us apart to do great things for the sake of the Gospel. You've entrusted us with souls and have given us the power to affect lives with our testimony. Today I just want to pause to thank You for the call You've placed on my child's life. I don't know where this road will take him, but I know that—like Barnabas and Saul—You have set him apart to do great and mighty things. Praise You, Father! Amen.

A Diligent Response

*Therefore, brothers, be all the more diligent to confirm your calling
and election, for if you practice these qualities you will never fall.
For in this way there will be richly provided for you an entrance
into the eternal kingdom of our Lord and Savior Jesus Christ.*
2 PETER 1:10–11 ESV

It's so easy to get excited about something when it's fresh and new,
Lord. I've seen this in my child's life. He dives into a particular sport,
so thrilled, and then loses heart. May he never lose heart when it comes
to the work You've called him to do, Lord. May he do as this verse
says: be diligent. Check and double-check where he stands with You.
Practice the qualities that prove he's got the spiritual goods. May his
diligence see him through the seasons when he feels like giving up,
Father. Help him, I pray. Amen.

Different Functions

*For just as each of us has one body with many members,
and these members do not all have the same function, so in Christ we,
though many, form one body, and each member belongs to all the others.*
ROMANS 12:4–5 NIV

I'm so glad You've made us all different, Lord. We're all part of the
same body (the church) but we're not all called to do exactly the same
things. I know this must be a huge relief to my child. She loves being
unique, different from the pack. She celebrates her individuality. What
a blessing to know that she's still part of the body and plays a role for
the greater good. We belong to each other, Father. Thank You for the
various roles we play. Amen.

You Called Us

*His divine power has granted to us all things that pertain
to life and godliness, through the knowledge of him
who called us to his own glory and excellence.*
2 PETER 1:3 ESV

I remember the old days, Lord, when our house had a telephone
(not a cell phone). When it rang, everyone rushed to answer it at
once. You never knew who might be on the other end of the line. It
could've been for anyone. I know that You have placed a call on each
of our lives—mine, my child's, the church body as a whole. We all
have an individual call, meant just for us. I pray that You would make
my child's "call" clear. May he answer the call, knowing it's meant just
for him, Lord. Amen.

Rich in Faith

*Listen, my beloved brothers, has not God chosen those
who are poor in the world to be rich in faith and heirs of
the kingdom, which he has promised to those who love him?*
JAMES 2:5 ESV

Sometimes my child feels insecure, Lord. Inferior. She sees all of her
flaws and not her gifts. When she thinks about being called to minister to other people, she cringes. Remind her today that You call all
of Your children to do a special work. You choose those who are "poor
of this world" (those who feel they're lacking) and make them rich in
faith. What she lacks in skill, You will more than make up for in grace,
Father. May she see her effectiveness as she draws close to You. Amen.

Reverent Service

*Therefore let us be grateful for receiving a kingdom
that cannot be shaken, and thus let us offer to God
acceptable worship, with reverence and awe.*
HEBREWS 12:28 ESV

Responding to Your call isn't something we take lightly, Lord. It's a life-changing decision. It has to be done with reverence and fear. Today, please help me as I share this information with my child. I want him to see the importance of responding to Your call on his life. May it not be just "one more thing" he has to do; may it be something that propels him to grow, to develop in his faith, and to step out in faith. Thank You for calling him, Lord. Amen.

A Moment

*When Jesus had called the Twelve together, he gave them power
and authority to drive out all demons and to cure diseases,
and he sent them out to proclaim the kingdom of God and to heal the sick.*
LUKE 9:1–2 NIV

There was a moment in time when You called together the twelve disciples, Lord, and gave them a specific "call" to do great things for You. That's what I'm praying for today. May my child have a "moment" with You, one that changes the course of her life. May she hear Your voice clearly as You call her out to do great and mighty things. May "the moment" change her thinking, her motivation, and her heart. Amen.

Delivered!

*For he has rescued us from the dominion of darkness
and brought us into the kingdom of the Son he loves,
in whom we have redemption, the forgiveness of sins.*
COLOSSIANS 1:13–14 NIV

So many people are living in darkness, Lord. That's why it's so important for us to respond to the call to go and preach the Gospel, so that lives can be changed and hope can be restored. It thrills me to think that my child will be a difference-maker in this dark world. Lives will be transformed as he spreads Your love, Your Word. Prepare his heart today to do amazing things for You, Father. Amen.

Go

*Now the LORD said to Abram, "Go from your country and your
kindred and your father's house to the land that I will show you."*
GENESIS 12:1 ESV

From the beginning of time, God has called his people to go. To leave the comfort of their own homes and travel to places they've never been. It's possible my child will one day leave the comfort of home, neighborhood, church, and community. The idea makes me cringe, Lord, but the possibility is there. You might call him to another state, or even another country. Wherever he settles, may he rest confident in the comfort of Your calling. Amen.

Chosen

"For many are called, but few are chosen."
MATTHEW 22:14 ESV

My child is not only called, Lord. He's chosen. That puts him in a narrower category, a smaller group. Those who are chosen have tasks yet to complete, roads to travel, dreams to fulfill. They have a mandate to touch lives, to minister to the hurting, to lift the name of Jesus to people they've not yet met. It's hard to remember all of this when I'm looking at his messy room and tossing his dirty socks in the dryer, Lord. Thanks for the reminder that he's got great things ahead. Amen.

Everywhere

And they went out and preached everywhere, while the Lord worked with them and confirmed the message by accompanying signs.
MARK 16:20 ESV

I'll be honest, Lord. . .when I read the word *everywhere* I cringe. I can hardly picture my child driving, let alone going to places across the globe that I've never even been to myself. Yet, I know she's called to reach people that I'll never reach. To love people I won't even know. You've placed a call on her life to go. . .and (hard as that might be to comprehend now) she will, indeed, go. Where? Only You know, Father, but I trust You to put her feet on the right path and to calm my heart when the time comes. Amen.

A Lifetime of Prayer

———

Our children won't always be young. It pains us to acknowledge this, but it's true. One day they will grow up, marry, and have children of their own. Along the way, our prayers will continue, though the topics will change. The updated list will include things like: driving lessons, dating, college plans, career, and marriage. Of course, we will spend just as much time praying for our grandbabies when the time comes, so our passionate prayers for our kids might be cut short as prayers for those darling grandbabies take precedence. What a joy that will be!

To many, the idea of grandchildren probably seems like a million light years away, but time whizzes by. Our parents would chime in with a resounding "Amen" at this notion. It seems we blink and our children are grown. So we must do all we can during this little window of time: Cover them in prayer. Teach them the things of the Lord. Encourage them when they make mistakes. . .all of these things are critical and timely. Our spiritual umbrellas must remain open at all times, providing the protection they need.

May our prayers for our children change their situations for the better. May they, as children of faith, change their world. What more could a parent could ask for, after all?

Read Thru the Bible in a Year

1-Jan	Gen. 1-2	Matt. 1	Ps. 1
2-Jan	Gen. 3-4	Matt. 2	Ps. 2
3-Jan	Gen. 5-7	Matt. 3	Ps. 3
4-Jan	Gen. 8-10	Matt. 4	Ps. 4
5-Jan	Gen. 11-13	Matt. 5:1-20	Ps. 5
6-Jan	Gen. 14-16	Matt. 5:21-48	Ps. 6
7-Jan	Gen. 17-18	Matt. 6:1-18	Ps. 7
8-Jan	Gen. 19-20	Matt. 6:19-34	Ps. 8
9-Jan	Gen. 21-23	Matt. 7:1-11	Ps. 9:1-8
10-Jan	Gen. 24	Matt. 7:12-29	Ps. 9:9-20
11-Jan	Gen. 25-26	Matt. 8:1-17	Ps. 10:1-11
12-Jan	Gen. 27:1-28:9	Matt. 8:18-34	Ps. 10:12-18
13-Jan	Gen. 28:10-29:35	Matt. 9	Ps. 11
14-Jan	Gen. 30:1-31:21	Matt. 10:1-15	Ps. 12
15-Jan	Gen. 31:22-32:21	Matt. 10:16-36	Ps. 13
16-Jan	Gen. 32:22-34:31	Matt. 10:37-11:6	Ps. 14
17-Jan	Gen. 35-36	Matt. 11:7-24	Ps. 15
18-Jan	Gen. 37-38	Matt. 11:25-30	Ps. 16
19-Jan	Gen. 39-40	Matt. 12:1-29	Ps. 17
20-Jan	Gen. 41	Matt. 12:30-50	Ps. 18:1-15
21-Jan	Gen. 42-43	Matt. 13:1-9	Ps. 18:16-29
22-Jan	Gen. 44-45	Matt. 13:10-23	Ps. 18:30-50
23-Jan	Gen. 46:1-47:26	Matt. 13:24-43	Ps. 19
24-Jan	Gen. 47:27-49:28	Matt. 13:44-58	Ps. 20
25-Jan	Gen. 49:29-Exod. 1:22	Matt. 14	Ps. 21
26-Jan	Exod. 2-3	Matt. 15:1-28	Ps. 22:1-21
27-Jan	Exod. 4:1-5:21	Matt. 15:29-16:12	Ps. 22:22-31
28-Jan	Exod. 5:22-7:24	Matt. 16:13-28	Ps. 23
29-Jan	Exod. 7:25-9:35	Matt. 17:1-9	Ps. 24
30-Jan	Exod. 10-11	Matt. 17:10-27	Ps. 25
31-Jan	Exod. 12	Matt. 18:1-20	Ps. 26
1-Feb	Exod. 13-14	Matt. 18:21-35	Ps. 27
2-Feb	Exod. 15-16	Matt. 19:1-15	Ps. 28
3-Feb	Exod. 17-19	Matt. 19:16-30	Ps. 29
4-Feb	Exod. 20-21	Matt. 20:1-19	Ps. 30
5-Feb	Exod. 22-23	Matt. 20:20-34	Ps. 31:1-8
6-Feb	Exod. 24-25	Matt. 21:1-27	Ps. 31:9-18
7-Feb	Exod 26-27	Matt. 21:28-46	Ps. 31:19-24
8-Feb	Exod. 28	Matt. 22	Ps. 32
9-Feb	Exod. 29	Matt. 23:1-36	Ps. 33:1-12
10-Feb	Exod. 30-31	Matt. 23:37-24:28	Ps. 33:13-22
11-Feb	Exod. 32-33	Matt. 24:29-51	Ps. 34:1-7
12-Feb	Exod. 34:1-35:29	Matt. 25:1-13	Ps. 34:8-22
13-Feb	Exod. 35:30-37:29	Matt. 25:14-30	Ps. 35:1-8
14-Feb	Exod. 38-39	Matt. 25:31-46	Ps. 35:9-17
15-Feb	Exod. 40	Matt. 26:1-35	Ps. 35:18-28
16-Feb	Lev. 1-3	Matt. 26:36-68	Ps. 36:1-6
17-Feb	Lev. 4:1-5:13	Matt. 26:69-27:26	Ps. 36:7-12
18-Feb	Lev. 5:14 -7:21	Matt. 27:27-50	Ps. 37:1-6

19-Feb	Lev. 7:22-8:36	Matt. 27:51-66	Ps. 37:7-26
20-Feb	Lev. 9-10	Matt. 28	Ps. 37:27-40
21-Feb	Lev. 11-12	Mark 1:1-28	Ps. 38
22-Feb	Lev. 13	Mark 1:29-39	Ps. 39
23-Feb	Lev. 14	Mark 1:40-2:12	Ps. 40:1-8
24-Feb	Lev. 15	Mark 2:13-3:35	Ps. 40:9-17
25-Feb	Lev. 16-17	Mark 4:1-20	Ps. 41:1-4
26-Feb	Lev. 18-19	Mark 4:21-41	Ps. 41:5-13
27-Feb	Lev. 20	Mark 5	Ps. 42-43
28-Feb	Lev. 21-22	Mark 6:1-13	Ps. 44
1-Mar	Lev. 23-24	Mark 6:14-29	Ps. 45:1-5
2-Mar	Lev. 25	Mark 6:30-56	Ps. 45:6-12
3-Mar	Lev. 26	Mark 7	Ps. 45:13-17
4-Mar	Lev. 27	Mark 8	Ps. 46
5-Mar	Num. 1-2	Mark 9:1-13	Ps. 47
6-Mar	Num. 3	Mark 9:14-50	Ps. 48:1-8
7-Mar	Num. 4	Mark 10:1-34	Ps. 48:9-14
8-Mar	Num. 5:1-6:21	Mark 10:35-52	Ps. 49:1-9
9-Mar	Num. 6:22-7:47	Mark 11	Ps. 49:10-20
10-Mar	Num. 7:48-8:4	Mark 12:1-27	Ps. 50:1-15
11-Mar	Num. 8:5-9:23	Mark 12:28-44	Ps. 50:16-23
12-Mar	Num. 10-11	Mark 13:1-8	Ps. 51:1-9
13-Mar	Num. 12-13	Mark 13:9-37	Ps. 51:10-19
14-Mar	Num. 14	Mark 14:1-31	Ps. 52
15-Mar	Num. 15	Mark 14:32-72	Ps. 53
16-Mar	Num. 16	Mark 15:1-32	Ps. 54
17-Mar	Num. 17-18	Mark 15:33-47	Ps. 55
18-Mar	Num. 19-20	Mark 16	Ps. 56:1-7
19-Mar	Num. 21:1-22:20	Luke 1:1-25	Ps. 56:8-13
20-Mar	Num. 22:21-23:30	Luke 1:26-56	Ps. 57
21-Mar	Num. 24-25	Luke 1:57-2:20	Ps. 58
22-Mar	Num. 26:1-27:11	Luke 2:21-38	Ps. 59:1-8
23-Mar	Num. 27:12-29:11	Luke 2:39-52	Ps. 59:9-17
24-Mar	Num. 29:12-30:16	Luke 3	Ps. 60:1-5
25-Mar	Num. 31	Luke 4	Ps. 60:6-12
26-Mar	Num. 32-33	Luke 5:1-16	Ps. 61
27-Mar	Num. 34-36	Luke 5:17-32	Ps. 62:1-6
28-Mar	Deut. 1:1-2:25	Luke 5:33-6:11	Ps. 62:7-12
29-Mar	Deut. 2:26-4:14	Luke 6:12-35	Ps. 63:1-5
30-Mar	Deut. 4:15-5:22	Luke 6:36-49	Ps. 63:6-11
31-Mar	Deut. 5:23-7:26	Luke 7:1-17	Ps. 64:1-5
1-Apr	Deut. 8-9	Luke 7:18-35	Ps. 64:6-10
2-Apr	Deut. 10-11	Luke 7:36-8:3	Ps. 65:1-8
3-Apr	Deut. 12-13	Luke 8:4-21	Ps. 65:9-13
4-Apr	Deut. 14:1-16:8	Luke 8:22-39	Ps. 66:1-7
5-Apr	Deut. 16:9-18:22	Luke 8:40-56	Ps. 66:8-15
6-Apr	Deut. 19:1-21:9	Luke 9:1-22	Ps. 66:16-20
7-Apr	Deut. 21:10-23:8	Luke 9:23-42	Ps. 67
8-Apr	Deut. 23:9-25:19	Luke 9:43-62	Ps. 68:1-6
9-Apr	Deut. 26:1-28:14	Luke 10:1-20	Ps. 68:7-14
10-Apr	Deut. 28:15-68	Luke 10:21-37	Ps. 68:15-19
11-Apr	Deut. 29-30	Luke 10:38-11:23	Ps. 68:20-27
12-Apr	Deut. 31:1-32:22	Luke 11:24-36	Ps. 68:28-35

13-Apr	Deut. 32:23-33:29	Luke 11:37-54	Ps. 69:1-9
14-Apr	Deut. 34-Josh. 2	Luke 12:1-15	Ps. 69:10-17
15-Apr	Josh. 3:1-5:12	Luke 12:16-40	Ps. 69:18-28
16-Apr	Josh. 5:13-7:26	Luke 12:41-48	Ps. 69:29-36
17-Apr	Josh. 8-9	Luke 12:49-59	Ps. 70
18-Apr	Josh. 10:1-11:15	Luke 13:1-21	Ps. 71:1-6
19-Apr	Josh. 11:16-13:33	Luke 13:22-35	Ps. 71:7-16
20-Apr	Josh. 14-16	Luke 14:1-15	Ps. 71:17-21
21-Apr	Josh. 17:1-19:16	Luke 14:16-35	Ps. 71:22-24
22-Apr	Josh. 19:17-21:42	Luke 15:1-10	Ps. 72:1-11
23-Apr	Josh. 21:43-22:34	Luke 15:11-32	Ps. 72:12-20
24-Apr	Josh. 23-24	Luke 16:1-18	Ps. 73:1-9
25-Apr	Judg. 1-2	Luke 16:19-17:10	Ps. 73:10-20
26-Apr	Judg. 3-4	Luke 17:11-37	Ps. 73:21-28
27-Apr	Judg. 5:1-6:24	Luke 18:1-17	Ps. 74:1-3
28-Apr	Judg. 6:25-7:25	Luke 18:18-43	Ps. 74:4-11
29-Apr	Judg. 8:1-9:23	Luke 19:1-28	Ps. 74:12-17
30-Apr	Judg. 9:24-10:18	Luke 19:29-48	Ps. 74:18-23
1-May	Judg. 11:1-12:7	Luke 20:1-26	Ps. 75:1-7
2-May	Judg. 12:8-14:20	Luke 20:27-47	Ps. 75:8-10
3-May	Judg. 15-16	Luke 21:1-19	Ps. 76:1-7
4-May	Judg. 17-18	Luke 21:20-22:6	Ps. 76:8-12
5-May	Judg. 19:1-20:23	Luke 22:7-30	Ps. 77:1-11
6-May	Judg. 20:24-21:25	Luke 22:31-54	Ps. 77:12-20
7-May	Ruth 1-2	Luke 22:55-23:25	Ps. 78:1-4
8-May	Ruth 3-4	Luke 23:26-24:12	Ps. 78:5-8
9-May	1 Sam. 1:1-2:21	Luke 24:13-53	Ps. 78:9-16
10-May	1 Sam. 2:22-4:22	John 1:1-28	Ps. 78:17-24
11-May	1 Sam. 5-7	John 1:29-51	Ps. 78:25-33
12-May	1 Sam. 8:1-9:26	John 2	Ps. 78:34-41
13-May	1 Sam. 9:27-11:15	John 3:1-22	Ps. 78:42-55
14-May	1 Sam. 12-13	John 3:23-4:10	Ps. 78:56-66
15-May	1 Sam. 14	John 4:11-38	Ps. 78:67-72
16-May	1 Sam. 15-16	John 4:39-54	Ps. 79:1-7
17-May	1 Sam. 17	John 5:1-24	Ps. 79:8-13
18-May	1 Sam. 18-19	John 5:25-47	Ps. 80:1-7
19-May	1 Sam. 20-21	John 6:1-21	Ps. 80:8-19
20-May	1 Sam. 22-23	John 6:22-42	Ps. 81:1-10
21-May	1 Sam. 24:1-25:31	John 6:43-71	Ps. 81:11-16
22-May	1 Sam. 25:32-27:12	John 7:1-24	Ps. 82
23-May	1 Sam. 28-29	John 7:25-8:11	Ps. 83
24-May	1 Sam. 30-31	John 8:12-47	Ps. 84:1-4
25-May	2 Sam. 1-2	John 8:48-9:12	Ps. 84:5-12
26-May	2 Sam. 3-4	John 9:13-34	Ps. 85:1-7
27-May	2 Sam. 5:1-7:17	John 9:35-10:10	Ps. 85:8-13
28-May	2 Sam. 7:18-10:19	John 10:11-30	Ps. 86:1-10
29-May	2 Sam. 11:1-12:25	John 10:31-11:16	Ps. 86:11-17
30-May	2 Sam. 12:26-13:39	John 11:17-54	Ps. 87
31-May	2 Sam. 14:1-15:12	John 11:55-12:19	Ps. 88:1-9
1-Jun	2 Sam. 15:13-16:23	John 12:20-43	Ps. 88:10-18
2-Jun	2 Sam. 17:1-18:18	John 12:44-13:20	Ps. 89:1-6
3-Jun	2 Sam. 18:19-19:39	John 13:21-38	Ps. 89:7-13
4-Jun	2 Sam. 19:40-21:22	John 14:1-17	Ps. 89:14-18

5-Jun	2 Sam. 22:1-23:7	John 14:18-15:27	Ps. 89:19-29
6-Jun	2 Sam. 23:8-24:25	John 16:1-22	Ps. 89:30-37
7-Jun	1 Kings 1	John 16:23-17:5	Ps. 89:38-52
8-Jun	1 Kings 2	John 17:6-26	Ps. 90:1-12
9-Jun	1 Kings 3-4	John 18:1-27	Ps. 90:13-17
10-Jun	1 Kings 5-6	John 18:28-19:5	Ps. 91:1-10
11-Jun	1 Kings 7	John 19:6-25a	Ps. 91:11-16
12-Jun	1 Kings 8:1-53	John 19:25b-42	Ps. 92:1-9
13-Jun	1 Kings 8:54-10:13	John 20:1-18	Ps. 92:10-15
14-Jun	1 Kings 10:14-11:43	John 20:19-31	Ps. 93
15-Jun	1 Kings 12:1-13:10	John 21	Ps. 94:1-11
16-Jun	1 Kings 13:11-14:31	Acts 1:1-11	Ps. 94:12-23
17-Jun	1 Kings 15:1-16:20	Acts 1:12-26	Ps. 95
18-Jun	1 Kings 16:21-18:19	Acts 2:1-21	Ps. 96:1-8
19-Jun	1 Kings 18:20-19:21	Acts2:22-41	Ps. 96:9-13
20-Jun	1 Kings 20	Acts 2:42-3:26	Ps. 97:1-6
21-Jun	1 Kings 21:1-22:28	Acts 4:1-22	Ps. 97:7-12
22-Jun	1 Kings 22:29- 2 Kings 1:18	Acts 4:23-5:11	Ps. 98
23-Jun	2 Kings 2-3	Acts 5:12-28	Ps. 99
24-Jun	2 Kings 4	Acts 5:29-6:15	Ps. 100
25-Jun	2 Kings 5:1-6:23	Acts 7:1-16	Ps. 101
26-Jun	2 Kings 6:24-8:15	Acts 7:17-36	Ps. 102:1-7
27-Jun	2 Kings 8:16-9:37	Acts 7:37-53	Ps. 102:8-17
28-Jun	2 Kings 10-11	Acts 7:54-8:8	Ps. 102:18-28
29-Jun	2 Kings 12-13	Acts 8:9-40	Ps. 103:1-9
30-Jun	2 Kings 14-15	Acts 9:1-16	Ps. 103:10-14
1-Jul	2 Kings 16-17	Acts 9:17-31	Ps. 103:15-22
2-Jul	2 Kings 18:1-19:7	Acts 9:32-10:16	Ps. 104:1-9
3-Jul	2 Kings 19:8-20:21	Acts 10:17-33	Ps. 104:10-23
4-Jul	2 Kings 21:1-22:20	Acts 10:34-11:18	Ps. 104: 24-30
5-Jul	2 Kings 23	Acts 11:19-12:17	Ps. 104:31-35
6-Jul	2 Kings 24-25	Acts 12:18-13:13	Ps. 105:1-7
7-Jul	1 Chron. 1-2	Acts 13:14-43	Ps. 105:8-15
8-Jul	1 Chron. 3:1-5:10	Acts 13:44-14:10	Ps. 105:16-28
9-Jul	1 Chron. 5:11-6:81	Acts 14:11-28	Ps. 105:29-36
10-Jul	1 Chron. 7:1-9:9	Acts 15:1-18	Ps. 105:37-45
11-Jul	1 Chron. 9:10-11:9	Acts 15:19-41	Ps. 106:1-12
12-Jul	1 Chron. 11:10-12:40	Acts 16:1-15	Ps. 106:13-27
13-Jul	1 Chron. 13-15	Acts 16:16-40	Ps. 106:28-33
14-Jul	1 Chron. 16-17	Acts 17:1-14	Ps. 106:34-43
15-Jul	1 Chron. 18-20	Acts 17:15-34	Ps. 106:44-48
16-Jul	1 Chron. 21-22	Acts 18:1-23	Ps. 107:1-9
17-Jul	1 Chron. 23-25	Acts 18:24-19:10	Ps. 107:10-16
18-Jul	1 Chron. 26-27	Acts 19:11-22	Ps. 107:17-32
19-Jul	1 Chron. 28-29	Acts 19:23-41	Ps. 107:33-38
20-Jul	2 Chron. 1-3	Acts 20:1-16	Ps. 107:39-43
21-Jul	2 Chron. 4:1-6:11	Acts 20:17-38	Ps. 108
22-Jul	2 Chron. 6:12-7:10	Acts 21:1-14	Ps. 109:1-20
23-Jul	2 Chron. 7:11-9:28	Acts 21:15-32	Ps. 109:21-31
24-Jul	2 Chron. 9:29-12:16	Acts 21:33-22:16	Ps. 110:1-3
25-Jul	2 Chron. 13-15	Acts 22:17-23:11	Ps. 110:4-7
26-Jul	2 Chron. 16-17	Acts 23:12-24:21	Ps. 111

18-Sep	Isa. 20-23	2 Cor. 6	Ps. 147:12-20
19-Sep	Isa. 24:1-26:19	2 Cor. 7	Ps. 148
20-Sep	Isa. 26:20-28:29	2 Cor. 8	Ps. 149-150
21-Sep	Isa. 29-30	2 Cor. 9	Prov. 1:1-9
22-Sep	Isa. 31-33	2 Cor. 10	Prov. 1:10-22
23-Sep	Isa. 34-36	2 Cor. 11	Prov. 1:23-26
24-Sep	Isa. 37-38	2 Cor. 12:1-10	Prov. 1:27-33
25-Sep	Isa. 39-40	2 Cor. 12:11-13:14	Prov. 2:1-15
26-Sep	Isa. 41-42	Gal. 1	Prov. 2:16-22
27-Sep	Isa. 43:1-44:20	Gal. 2	Prov. 3:1-12
28-Sep	Isa. 44:21-46:13	Gal. 3:1-18	Prov. 3:13-26
29-Sep	Isa. 47:1-49:13	Gal 3:19-29	Prov. 3:27-35
30-Sep	Isa. 49:14-51:23	Gal 4:1-11	Prov. 4:1-19
1-Oct	Isa. 52-54	Gal. 4:12-31	Prov. 4:20-27
2-Oct	Isa. 55-57	Gal. 5	Prov. 5:1-14
3-Oct	Isa. 58-59	Gal. 6	Prov. 5:15-23
4-Oct	Isa. 60-62	Eph. 1	Prov. 6:1-5
5-Oct	Isa. 63:1-65:16	Eph. 2	Prov. 6:6-19
6-Oct	Isa. 65:17-66:24	Eph. 3:1-4:16	Prov. 6:20-26
7-Oct	Jer. 1-2	Eph. 4:17-32	Prov. 6:27-35
8-Oct	Jer. 3:1-4:22	Eph. 5	Prov. 7:1-5
9-Oct	Jer. 4:23-5:31	Eph. 6	Prov. 7:6-27
10-Oct	Jer. 6:1-7:26	Phil. 1:1-26	Prov. 8:1-11
11-Oct	Jer. 7:26-9:16	Phil. 1:27-2:18	Prov. 8:12-21
12-Oct	Jer. 9:17-11:17	Phil 2:19-30	Prov. 8:22-36
13-Oct	Jer. 11:18-13:27	Phil. 3	Prov. 9:1-6
14-Oct	Jer. 14-15	Phil. 4	Prov. 9:7-18
15-Oct	Jer. 16-17	Col. 1:1-23	Prov. 10:1-5
16-Oct	Jer. 18:1-20:6	Col. 1:24-2:15	Prov. 10:6-14
17-Oct	Jer. 20:7-22:19	Col. 2:16-3:4	Prov. 10:15-26
18-Oct	Jer. 22:20-23:40	Col. 3:5-4:1	Prov. 10:27-32
19-Oct	Jer. 24-25	Col. 4:2-18	Prov. 11:1-11
20-Oct	Jer. 26-27	1 Thes. 1:1-2:8	Prov. 11:12-21
21-Oct	Jer. 28-29	1 Thes. 2:9-3:13	Prov. 11:22-26
22-Oct	Jer. 30:1-31:22	1 Thes. 4:1-5:11	Prov. 11:27-31
23-Oct	Jer. 31:23-32:35	1 Thes. 5:12-28	Prov. 12:1-14
24-Oct	Jer. 32:36-34:7	2 Thes. 1-2	Prov. 12:15-20
25-Oct	Jer. 34:8-36:10	2 Thes. 3	Prov. 12:21-28
26-Oct	Jer. 36:11-38:13	1 Tim. 1:1-17	Prov. 13:1-4
27-Oct	Jer. 38:14-40:6	1 Tim. 1:18-3:13	Prov. 13:5-13
28-Oct	Jer. 40:7-42:22	1 Tim. 3:14-4:10	Prov. 13:14-21
29-Oct	Jer. 43-44	1 Tim. 4:11-5:16	Prov. 13:22-25
30-Oct	Jer. 45-47	1 Tim. 5:17-6:21	Prov. 14:1-6
31-Oct	Jer. 48:1-49:6	2 Tim. 1	Prov. 14:7-22
1-Nov	Jer. 49:7-50:16	2 Tim. 2	Prov. 14:23-27
2-Nov	Jer. 50:17-51:14	2 Tim. 3	Prov. 14:28-35
3-Nov	Jer. 51:15-64	2 Tim. 4	Prov. 15:1-9
4-Nov	Jer. 52-Lam. 1	Ti. 1:1-9	Prov. 15:10-17
5-Nov	Lam. 2:1-3:38	Ti. 1:10-2:15	Prov. 15:18-26
6-Nov	Lam. 3:39-5:22	Ti. 3	Prov. 15:27-33
7-Nov	Ezek. 1:1-3:21	Philemon 1	Prov. 16:1-9
8-Nov	Ezek. 3:22-5:17	Heb. 1:1-2:4	Prov. 16:10-21
9-Nov	Ezek. 6-7	Heb. 2:5-18	Prov. 16:22-33

10-Nov	Ezek. 8-10	Heb. 3:1-4:3	Prov. 17:1-5
11-Nov	Ezek. 11-12	Heb. 4:4-5:10	Prov. 17:6-12
12-Nov	Ezek. 13-14	Heb. 5:11-6:20	Prov. 17:13-22
13-Nov	Ezek. 15:1-16:43	Heb. 7:1-28	Prov. 17:23-28
14-Nov	Ezek. 16:44-17:24	Heb. 8:1-9:10	Prov. 18:1-7
15-Nov	Ezek. 18-19	Heb. 9:11-28	Prov. 18:8-17
16-Nov	Ezek. 20	Heb. 10:1-25	Prov. 18:18-24
17-Nov	Ezek. 21-22	Heb. 10:26-39	Prov. 19:1-8
18-Nov	Ezek. 23	Heb. 11:1-31	Prov. 19:9-14
19-Nov	Ezek. 24-26	Heb. 11:32-40	Prov. 19:15-21
20-Nov	Ezek. 27-28	Heb. 12:1-13	Prov. 19:22-29
21-Nov	Ezek. 29-30	Heb. 12:14-29	Prov. 20:1-18
22-Nov	Ezek. 31-32	Heb. 13	Prov. 20:19-24
23-Nov	Ezek. 33:1-34:10	Jas. 1	Prov. 20:25-30
24-Nov	Ezek. 34:11-36:15	Jas. 2	Prov. 21:1-8
25-Nov	Ezek. 36:16-37:28	Jas. 3	Prov. 21:9-18
26-Nov	Ezek. 38-39	Jas. 4:1-5:6	Prov. 21:19-24
27-Nov	Ezek. 40	Jas. 5:7-20	Prov. 21:25-31
28-Nov	Ezek. 41:1-43:12	1 Pet. 1:1-12	Prov. 22:1-9
29-Nov	Ezek. 43:13-44:31	1 Pet. 1:13-2:3	Prov. 22:10-23
30-Nov	Ezek. 45-46	1 Pet. 2:4-17	Prov. 22:24-29
1-Dec	Ezek. 47-48	1 Pet. 2:18-3:7	Prov. 23:1-9
2-Dec	Dan. 1:1-2:23	1 Pet. 3:8-4:19	Prov. 23:10-16
3-Dec	Dan. 2:24-3:30	1 Pet. 5	Prov. 23:17-25
4-Dec	Dan. 4	2 Pet. 1	Prov. 23:26-35
5-Dec	Dan. 5	2 Pet. 2	Prov. 24:1-18
6-Dec	Dan. 6:1-7:14	2 Pet. 3	Prov. 24:19-27
7-Dec	Dan. 7:15-8:27	1 John 1:1-2:17	Prov. 24:28-34
8-Dec	Dan. 9-10	1 John 2:18-29	Prov. 25:1-12
9-Dec	Dan. 11-12	1 John 3:1-12	Prov. 25:13-17
10-Dec	Hos. 1-3	1 John 3:13-4:16	Prov. 25:18-28
11-Dec	Hos. 4-6	1 John 4:17-5:21	Prov. 26:1-16
12-Dec	Hos. 7-10	2 John	Prov. 26:17-21
13-Dec	Hos. 11-14	3 John	Prov. 26:22-27:9
14-Dec	Joel 1:1-2:17	Jude	Prov. 27:10-17
15-Dec	Joel 2:18-3:21	Rev. 1:1-2:11	Prov. 27:18-27
16-Dec	Amos 1:1-4:5	Rev. 2:12-29	Prov. 28:1-8
17-Dec	Amos 4:6-6:14	Rev. 3	Prov. 28:9-16
18-Dec	Amos 7-9	Rev. 4:1-5:5	Prov. 28:17-24
19-Dec	Obad-Jonah	Rev. 5:6-14	Prov. 28:25-28
20-Dec	Mic. 1:1-4:5	Rev. 6:1-7:8	Prov. 29:1-8
21-Dec	Mic. 4:6-7:20	Rev. 7:9-8:13	Prov. 29:9-14
22-Dec	Nah. 1-3	Rev. 9-10	Prov. 29:15-23
23-Dec	Hab. 1-3	Rev. 11	Prov. 29:24-27
24-Dec	Zeph. 1-3	Rev. 12	Prov. 30:1-6
25-Dec	Hag. 1-2	Rev. 13:1-14:13	Prov. 30:7-16
26-Dec	Zech. 1-4	Rev. 14:14-16:3	Prov. 30:17-20
27-Dec	Zech. 5-8	Rev. 16:4-21	Prov. 30:21-28
28-Dec	Zech. 9-11	Rev. 17:1-18:8	Prov. 30:29-33
29-Dec	Zech. 12-14	Rev. 18:9-24	Prov. 31:1-9
30-Dec	Mal. 1-2	Rev. 19-20	Prov. 31:10-17
31-Dec	Mal. 3-4	Rev. 21-22	Prov. 31:18-31